Study Guide with Map Exercises
for use with

The Unfinished Nation
A Concise History of the American People

Fourth Edition

Volume I

Alan Brinkley
Columbia University

Prepared by
Harvey H. Jackson
Jacksonville State University

Bradley R. Rice
Clayton College & State University

Boston   Burr Ridge, IL   Dubuque, IA   Madison, WI   New York   San Francisco   St. Louis
Bangkok   Bogotá   Caracas   Kuala Lumpur   Lisbon   London   Madrid   Mexico City
Milan   Montreal   New Delhi   Santiago   Seoul   Singapore   Sydney   Taipei   Toronto

The *McGraw·Hill* Companies

McGraw-Hill Higher Education

A Division of The McGraw-Hill Companies

Study Guide with Map Exercises Volume I for use with
THE UNFINISHED NATION
Alan Brinkley

Published by McGraw-Hill, an imprint of The McGraw-Hill Companies, Inc.,
1221 Avenue of the Americas, New York, NY 10020. Copyright
© 2004 (2000, 1997, 1993) by The McGraw-Hill Companies, Inc.
All rights reserved.

1 2 3 4 5 6 7 8 9 0 BKM/BKM 0 9 8 7 6 5 4 3 2 1

ISBN 0-07-284694-1

www.mhhe.com

ABOUT THE AUTHORS

Harvey H. Jackson received his Ph.D. from the University of Georgia. With Bradley R. Rice, he wrote *Georgia: Empire State of the South*. He authored or coauthored books on early America, including *Lachlan McIntosh and the Politics of Revolutionary Georgia* (1979), and is now focusing his studies on the cultural environment of the South. In 1995 he published *Rivers of History: Life on the Coosa, Tallapoosa, Cahaba, and Alabama*, and in 1997 he published *Putting 'Loafing Streams' to Work: The Building of Lay, Mitchell, Martin and Jordan Dams, 1910–1929*. Jackson is currently working on a study of the northern coast of the Gulf of Mexico since World War II. His articles have appeared in several anthologies and journals including the *Journal of Southern History* and the *William and Mary Quarterly*. Harvey Jackson is Professor and Head of the Department of History and Foreign Languages at Jacksonville State University, Jacksonville, Alabama.

Bradley R. Rice received his Ph.D. from the University of Texas at Austin. He coauthored *Georgia: Empire State of the South* with Harvey H. Jackson and wrote *Progressive Cities: The Commission Government Movement in America, 1901–1920* (1977). Rice is coauthor and coeditor of *Sunbelt Cities: Politics and Growth Since World War II* (1983), and his work has appeared in several edited collections and journals including the *Journal of Urban History*. Since 1982, Rice has been editor of *Atlanta History: A Journal of Georgia and the South*, which is published quarterly by the Atlanta Historical Society. Rice is Professor of History and Assistant Vice President for Academic Affairs at Clayton State College, Morrow, Georgia.

TABLE OF CONTENTS

Introduction

Every history professor has heard hundreds of students complain that history is nothing but dry, irrelevant facts, names and dates to be memorized quickly and just as quickly forgotten. To be sure, for students to have a good framework of historical understanding, they must have a basic knowledge of factual information, but history is much more than that. Names and dates are really people and time. History is society's memory, and society cannot function without history any more than an individual could function without his or her memory. The names represent real flesh-and-blood people, both famous and common, and the dates mark the time when those people lived and worked. This study guide will try to lead you toward developing a historical perspective. You will be encouraged to go beyond the bare facts to think critically about the causes and consequences of historical decisions. Careful study of this guide in consultation with your instructor will help you use the text to its best advantage. With the guide, you can constantly test yourself to make sure that you have learned from what you have read.

Each chapter of the guide is composed of several parts: Objectives, Pertinent Questions, Identification, Document, Map Exercise, Summary, and a Self-Test. Your instructor may assign specific items from the guide that best complement his or her approach to the course, or you may be expected to use the guide on your own. It will work well with either approach. The guide is not a workbook or a shortcut. It does not recapitulate, outline, or simplify the work of Professor Brinkley. Rather, it is designed to challenge you to seek a better comprehension of the text in particular and American history in general.

It is best to look over the appropriate chapter in the guide before you read your assignment so that you will be better attuned to what to look for as you read. The objectives that are listed at the beginning of each chapter of the study guide will give you a general idea of what the chapter is about. The Identification items are important names and terms covered in the text but not usually directly mentioned in the Pertinent Questions section of the study guide. Of course, your instructor may add to and/or delete from these lists to meet the needs of the course.

The Pertinent Questions and the Self-Test questions are the heart of the study guide. The goal of these exercises is to provide you with a thoughtful method for self-assessment after you have read each chapter. Some students will wish to write out their answers in full; some will jot down a few key ideas; and others will simply check themselves "in their heads." Experiment and use whichever method works best for you (assuming it is acceptable to your instructor). You should keep in mind that no general survey text could possibly cover all the pertinent questions in American history or fully explicate those it does discuss. Do not become too preoccupied with incidental supporting detail. Look for the essence of the answer, and then seek out those facts and examples that support your conclusions.

The Document exercises in each chapter provide an opportunity for you to discover how important the analysis of documents can be to the historian's task. The questions about each document should be treated much like the Pertinent Questions. The Map Exercises let you see how geography can help you form a historical perspective.

At the end of the guide are sections that will help you write a critical book review or research paper if your instructor so requires. Such assignments will give you the opportunity to exercise critical thinking skills and apply the historical perspective that you have cultivated while reading the text and using this guide.

Naturally, this all seems like a drawn-out process, and at first it may well be. But as you work at it, you will find that each chapter will take less time, until finally you will have developed a system of study habits and analysis that will serve you well in this course and in many others as well.

Harvey H. Jackson
Bradley R. Rice

CHAPTER ONE

The Meeting of Cultures

OBJECTIVES

A thorough study of Chapter 1 should enable you to understand:

1. What the New World was like at the time of Christopher Columbus.
2. The ways in which the peoples of the New and Old Worlds affected each other when their societies came in contact in the late fifteenth century.
3. The colonial policies of the colonizing nations, and the effect each had on the future of the Americas.
4. Some important aspects of the culture from which Negro slaves were taken.
5. The early development of slavery.
6. The role of religion in European efforts to colonize the New World.
7. How the New World fit into the Atlantic World.
8. The first efforts of the English to establish a colony and the reasons for their failure.

PERTINENT QUESTIONS

America Before Columbus (pp. 4–7)

1. Identify and describe the elaborate native civilizations that developed in South and Central America and in Mexico.
2. Describe the way of life of the North American Indians—where they lived and how they supported themselves.
3. Describe the changes taking place among North American Indians during the century before Europeans arrived.
4. How were efforts to determine the pre-Columbian population of America tied to the larger debate over the consequences of European settlement of the Western Hemisphere?

Europe Looks Westward (pp. 7–19)

5. What changes stimulated Europeans to look toward new lands?
6. What did Columbus hope to achieve through his voyages, and what did he actually accomplish?
7. Why did the *conquistadores* seek to eliminate the underpinnings of existing American civilizations? How was this destruction accomplished?
8. Explain the relationship between the Spanish and the Pueblo Indians. How did this relationship shape the development of New Mexico?
9. Describe the demographic differences between the Spanish Empire in America and the empires to the north. What impact did European diseases have on colonization efforts?
10. What did Europeans gain from the Indians that proved more important than gold?
11. What did the intermarriage of Spanish and North Americans reveal about the Spanish colonial system and suggest about the Europeans who administered it?
12. What role did the Catholic Church play in Spanish colonization efforts?
13. Describe the cultures from which African slaves were taken and brought to America.
14. How did the African slave trade originate, and how did it evolve?
15. In what ways did the New World play a part in the development of the Atlantic World?

The Arrival of the English (pp. 19–24)

16. What commercial factors contributed to England's decision to seek colonies in the New World?
17. How did the English Reformation differ from that of Luther and Calvin? Why did it fail to satisfy the religious desires of many English people?
18. What did the Puritans wish to accomplish, and why did they clash with James I?
19. How did the English colonization of Ireland influence the way in which the English colonized America?
20. Where did the French and Dutch establish colonies in North America, and how did their efforts differ from those of the Spanish and the English?
21. What inspired the English to get into the race for colonies?

22. Describe the colonization efforts of Sir Humphrey Gilbert and Sir Walter Raleigh.
23. How did James I settle the rivalry between London and Plymouth merchants over the exploration of North America?

IDENTIFICATION

Identify each of the following, and explain why it is important within the context of the chapter.

1. Tenochtitlàn
2. Iroquois Confederation
3. Francisco Pizarro
4. mestizos
5. Mali
6. John Cabot
7. encomiendas
8. mercantilism
9. Separatists
10. coureurs de bois

DOCUMENT

John Smith is one of the most famous names associated with the English colonization of America, and his writings did much to introduce Europeans to America and to promote English colonization efforts. The document that follows is from his *General Historie of Virginia, New England, and the Summer Isles. . .* (1624), a chronicle of English exploration that drew heavily on the earlier work of Richard Hakluyt. This account of a meeting in 1584 between English explorers and Indians, although seen through the eyes of the English, tells us much about Indian life before the transformation of the tribes was complete. While reading it, consider the culture and possessions of the Indians and the English attitude toward what the Indians obviously valued. Also pay particular attention to what the English noticed about the Indians, and speculate on why these things were important to them.

> Till the third day we saw not any of the people, then in a little Boat three of them appeared, one of them went on shore, to whome wee rowed, and he attended vs without any signe of feare; after he had spoke much though we vnderstood not a word, of his owne accord he came boldly aboord vs, we gaue him a shirt, a hat, wine and meate, which he liked well, and after he had well viewed the barkes and vs, he went away in his owne Boat, and within a quarter of a myle of vs in halfe an houre, had loaden his Boat with fish, with which he came againe to the poynt of land, and there devided it in two parts, poynting one part to the Ship, the other part to the Pinnace, and so departed.

The next day came diuers Boats, and in one of them the Kings Brother, with forty or fifty men, proper people, and in their behauiour very ciuill; his name was *Granganameo*, the King is called *Winginia*, the Country *Wingandacoa*. Leauing his Boats a little from our Ships, he came with his trayne to the poynt: where spreading a Matte he sat downe. Though we came to him well armed, he made signes to vs to sit downe without any shew of feare, stroking his head and brest, and also ours, to expresse his loue. After he had made a long speech vnto vs, we presented him with diuers toyes, which he kindly accepted. He was greatly regarded by his people, for none of them did sit, nor speake a word, but foure, on whom we bestowed presents also, but he tooke all from them, making signes all things did belong to him.

The King himselfe in a conflict with a King his next neighbour and mortall enemy, was shot in two places through the body, and the thigh, yet recouered: whereby he lay at his chiefe towne six days journey from thence.

A day or two after shewing them what we had, *Granganameo* taking most liking to a Pewter dish, made a hole in it, hung it about his necke for a brestplate: for which he gaue vs twenty Deere skins, worth twenty Crownes; and for a Copper Kettell, fiftie skins, worth fiftie Crownes. Much other trucke we had, and after two dayes he came aboard, and did eate and drinke with vs very merrily. Not long after he brought his wife and children, they were but of meane stature, but well fauoured and very bashfull; she had a long coat of Leather, and about her priuities a peece of the same, about her forehead a band of white Corrall, and so had her husband, in her eares were bracelets of pearle, hanging downe to her middle, of the bignesse of great Pease; the rest of the women had Pendants of Copper, and the Noblemen fiue or six in an eare; his apparrell as his wiues, onely the women weare their haire long on both sides, and the men but on one; they are of colour yellow, but their hayre is blacke, yet we saw children that had very fayre Chestnut coloured hayre.

After that these women had beene here with vs, there came downe from all parts great stores of people, with Leather, Corrall, and diuers kinde of dyes, but when *Granganameo* was present, none durst trade but himselfe, and them that wore red Copper on their heads, as he did. When euer he came, he would signifie by so many fires he came with so many boats, that we might know his strength. Their Boats are but one great tree, which is but burnt in the forme of a trough with gins and fire, till it be as they would haue it. For an armour he would haue ingaged vs a bagge of pearle, but we refused, as not regarding it, that wee might the better learn where it grew. He was very iust of his promise, for oft we trusted him, and he would come within his day to keepe his word. He sent vs commonly euery day a brace of Bucks, Conies, Hares, and fish, sometimes Mellons, Walnuts, Cucumbers, Pease, and diuers roots. This Author sayeth, their come groweth three times in fiue moneths; in May they sow, in Iuly reape; in Iune they sow, in August reape; in Iuly sow, in August reape. We put some of our Pease in the ground, which in ten dayes were 14 ynches high.

John Smith, *Works*, ed. Edward Arber (Birmingham, Eng.: J. Grant, 1884), pp. 306–308.

MAP EXERCISE

Fill in or identify the following on the blank map provided. Use the maps on pages 6, 9, and 13 of the text as your source.

1. The routes of exploration, and the nations that sponsored these ventures.

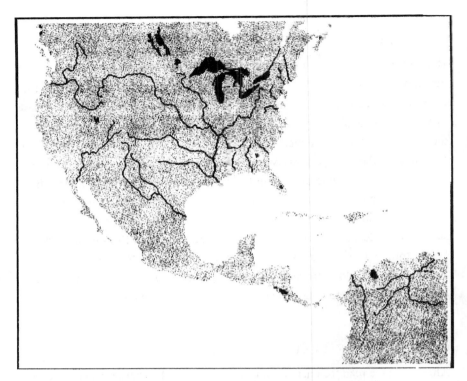

2. The principal Indian civilizations in North and Central America and in the Caribbean.
3. The centers of European settlement in North and Central America and in the Caribbean.

Interpretative Questions

Based on what you have filled in, answer the following. For some of the questions you will need to consult the narrative in your text for information or explanation.

1. In light of the European rivalries of the period, and considering the various areas explored, settled, or claimed by the various European nations, what potentials for conflict among them existed?
2. Still considering the areas explored by European rivals, what opportunities for intercolonial trade existed? For trade with the Indians? What might have prevented this trade from taking place?
3. Note the location of the Spanish missions. How might they have served a purpose other than religious? Why were forts often found with missions?
4. Consider the location of Spanish missions and forts. How might these have been sources of potential conflict with other European powers?

SUMMARY

Before European explorers arrived in the Americas, Native Americans had developed many forms of social organizations that differed from one another in their levels of achievement. Europeans, concerned first with exploiting the New World and its peoples, regarded the natives as savages and set out to destroy their societies and replace them with a variation of European culture. Helped in this quest by the biological disaster brought on by smallpox and other diseases, the Europeans were able to conquer the tribes and civilizations and impose on the Indians a number of different colonial systems. To help make up for the Indians' labor lost through conquest and epidemic, Europeans brought in African slaves, who added to the cultural diversity of America. Conflicts in the Old World spilled over into the New as different nations got into the race for colonies. By the end of the sixteenth century, the age of discovery was all but over, and the great era of colonization, especially English colonization, was about to begin.

CHAPTER SELF-TEST

After you have read the chapter in the text and done the exercises in the study guide, the following self-test can be taken to see if you understand the material you have covered. Answers appear at the end of the study guide.

Multiple Choice

Circle the letter of the response that best answers the question or completes the statement.

1. The Indian empire that dominated modern Mexico at the time of the Spanish conquest was the:
   a. Mayan.
   b. Inca.
   c. Aztec.
   d. Chaco.

2. At the time of the Spanish conquest, the economies of most of the Native Americans in South and Central America and Mexico were based on:
   a. hunting and gathering.
   b. herding.
   c. fishing and gathering.
   d. agriculture.

3. The eastern third of what is now the United States was inhabited by the:
   a. Woodland Indians.
   b. Plains Indians.
   c. Mountain Indians.
   d. Coastal Tribes.

4. At least partly as a result of Columbus's voyages, Spain:
   a. got involved in the Indian slave trade.
   b. soon went to war with France.
   c. replaced Portugal as the foremost seafaring nation.
   d. opened trade with the great khan in China.

5. Through a combination of daring, brutality, and greed, the *conquistadores*:
   a. made possible the creation of a Spanish Empire in America.
   b. brought capitalism to Mexico.
   c. founded St. Augustine.
   d. introduced African slavery into America.

6. The first and perhaps most profound result of the meeting of native and European cultures was the:
   a. exchange of plants and animals.
   b. importation of European diseases.
   c. native adoption of European ways of waging war.
   d. intermarriage of Europeans and natives.

7. Ultimately more important to Europe than the gold and silver found in the New World was the:
   a. importation of new crops that could feed larger numbers of people.
   b. discovery of new forms of religious worship.
   c. Indian labor force.
   d. architectural knowledge gained from the Aztecs.

8. In matrilineal Indian and African societies:
   a. the father is the sole authority in the family.
   b. local gods were the basis of religious beliefs.
   c. women played a major, often dominant, role.
   d. slavery did not exist.

9. The African slave trade began:
   a. in the fifteenth century, soon after the Spanish conquest.
   b. as early as the eighth century.
   c. with the English settlement of Virginia.
   d. when the sugar industry moved to the Caribbean.

7

10. Which of the following was *not* an English incentive for colonization:
    a. to escape religious strife at home.
    b. to bring the Christian religion to the Indians.
    c. to escape the economic transformation of the countryside.
    d. to find new markets for English products.

11. According to the theory of mercantilism, a nation could be made strong by:
    a. exporting more than it imported.
    b. building up a large standing army.
    c. defeating its neighbors in war.
    d. importing more than it exported.

12. Members of the Church of England who claimed that the church had not given up Rome's offensive beliefs and practices were the:
    a. Baptists.
    b. Presbyterians.
    c. Methodists.
    d. Puritans.

13. The country that produced the most successful fur traders and trappers was:
    a. Spain.
    b. Holland.
    c. France.
    d. Germany.

14. The first permanent English settlement was:
    a. Massachusetts Bay.
    b. Jamestown, Virginia.
    c. Plymouth, Massachusetts.
    d. St. Augustine.

15. The man to whom Queen Elizabeth granted the land on which the "lost colony" was planted was:
    a. John White.
    b. Walter Raleigh.
    c. Humphrey Gilbert.
    d. James Cobb.

True/False

Read each statement carefully. Mark true statements "T" and false statements "F."

___1. The Aztec capital built on the site of present-day Mexico City was Cuzco.

___2. The large Indian trading center in the Mississippi River Valley near present day St. Louis was Cahokia.

___3. The Iroquois Confederation consisted of tribes in the southernmost region of the eastern seaboard.

___4. Cortés might not have been able to defeat the Aztecs had it not been for an epidemic of smallpox that decimated the native population.

___5. The oldest permanent European settlement in the present-day United States was St. Augustine.

___6. New Mexico became one of the most important provinces in Spanish America.

___7. The riches of America ultimately hurt Spain because they caused that country to ignore domestic economic growth.

___8. The most important Native American crop brought back by the Europeans was squash.

___9. Europeans felt justified in their treatment of the Indians because they considered the Indians uncivilized savages.

___10. Spaniards seldom intermarried with the Native Americans.

___11. Today it is generally believed that there were fewer Native Americans when the Europeans arrived than there were a century later.

___12. Mercantilism was a theory that discouraged nations from having colonies.

___13. Joint-stock companies were the means by which investors could share the risks and the profits of colonizing ventures.

___14. The doctrine that God "elected" some people to be saved and condemned others to damnation was preached by Martin Luther.

___15. The English Reformation began with a political dispute between king and pope—not with a religious dispute over matters of theology.

___16. England's first experience with colonization was in Virginia.

___17. The first Europeans to settle in the Hudson River Valley were the Dutch.

___18. In 1606, James I gave the exclusive right to colonize along the southeast coast to a group of London merchants.

Review Questions

These questions are to be answered with essays. This will allow you to explore relationships among individuals, events, and attitudes of the period under review.

1. Describe the Indian societies and their geographic distribution before the coming of the European explorers. What did these cultures contribute to the Europeans, and why, despite these contributions, did the invaders still think of the American Indians as savages?
2. Compare and contrast the Spanish and the English motives for colonization. How were both sets of motives reflected in the organization of the colonies that each nation established?
3. How did earlier exploration and colonization experiences influence the way England, Spain, and other European nations attempted to colonize America?
4. Explain the relationship between Spanish colonists and the Indians. Why did the Indians come out the losers?
5. Describe the social and cultural backgrounds of the Africans brought to America. How were these backgrounds different from Indians? Europeans? How were the backgrounds of these people alike?
6. How did the New World develop within the context of what has become known as the Atlantic World?

CHAPTER TWO

Transplantations and Borderlands

OBJECTIVES

A thorough study of Chapter 2 should enable you to understand:

1. The differences between the Jamestown and Plymouth colonies in terms of objectives, type of settlers, early problems, and reasons for success.
2. The causes and significance of Bacon's Rebellion.
3. The settlement of England's Caribbean colonies and why these provinces were significant.
4. The background of the Massachusetts Bay colony and its founders, the Puritans.
5. The conditions in Puritan Massachusetts Bay that spawned such dissenters as Roger Williams and Anne Hutchinson.
6. The reasons for the founding of each of the original thirteen colonies.
7. The early economic, religious, and political factors in the colonies that tended to produce sectional differences.
8. The effect of the Glorious Revolution on the development of the American colonies.

PERTINENT QUESTIONS

The Early Chesapeake (pp. 28–35)

1. What four conditions shaped the character of English settlements in America?
2. What serious difficulties did the Virginia colonists face from the moment they landed?
3. How did the motives of the Virginia colonists differ from those of the separatists who settled in Plymouth?
4. Explain the importance of tobacco in the development of the Virginia colony.
5. Explain how exchanges of agricultural technology between Europeans and Native Americans helped Jamestown survive.
6. What led to Virginia's becoming a royal colony?

7. What were the origins of the colony of Maryland? How did Maryland's early development differ from that of Virginia?
8. What were the origins of the political turmoil in Virginia during the 1670s?
9. How was Bacon's Rebellion related to the political unrest in Virginia, and what effect did the rebellion have on the development of that colony?

The Growth of New England (pp. 36–42)

10. Describe the background of the Pilgrims and their motives for coming to America.
11. How did the Pilgrims' experience with the Indians differ markedly from that of the settlers in Virginia?
12. How did the turbulent events in England generate interest in colonization among certain English Puritans? What did these Puritans hope to accomplish?
13. How did the charter of the Massachusetts Bay Company influence the colony's first government?
14. What did the Puritans believe to be their purpose in coming to America (their "mission"), and how did church and state cooperate to achieve this goal?
15. How did the colony of Connecticut originate? Rhode Island? What does this expansion ("exodus") reveal about the colony of Massachusetts Bay?
16. What was the controversy surrounding Anne Hutchinson, and what does it reveal about Puritan religious and social beliefs?
17. What factors made relations between Indians and colonists in New England such a disaster for Native Americans?
18. What obstacles did the colonists have to overcome if they were to be successful in America?
19. How were conflicts between natives and settlers affected by earlier exchanges in technology between the English and the tribes?

The Restoration Colonies (pp. 42–54)

20. How did the Stuart Restoration affect those English colonies already established in America? How did it affect attitudes about founding more settlements?
21. How did the political, economic, social, and religious institutions established in Carolina reflect the proprietors' motives for starting the colony?
22. What sort of social order took root in the colony of Carolina? Why did it differ from that proposed under Carolina's Fundamental Constitution?

23. How did the existing Dutch settlements and institutions influence the development of New York?
24. What beliefs and practices characterized the Quakers, and how did their influence make Pennsylvania a unique colony?
25. Why were the Caribbean colonies the "most important destinations" for English immigrants throughout the first half of the seventeenth century?
26. What circumstances led to English colonization in the Caribbean?
27. What conditions led English planters to begin importing labor to the Caribbean islands?
28. Why did Caribbean planters fear slave revolts? What steps did they take to prevent uprisings?
29. Why was it difficult to establish a stable society and culture in the Caribbean colonies?
30. Which colonies made up the Spanish borderlands and what sort of people settled there?
31. What role did the Spanish borderlands play in Spanish relations with England?
32. How did the purposes for which Georgia was founded differ from those of previous colonies? How were they similar?
33. What were the Middle Grounds? Which groups competed for them and what role did competition for this land play in the settlement and development of colonial North America?

The Development of Empire (pp. 54–56)

34. What attempts did England make to regulate its colonies between 1660 and 1700? What moved the mother country to consider regulation at this time, and how was it enforced?
35. What were the origins of the Dominion of New England, and what was the colonial reaction to it?
36. What impact did the Glorious Revolution have on England's North American colonies?

IDENTIFICATION

Identify each of the following, and explain why it is important within the context of the chapter.

1. "starving time"
2. John Rolfe
3. headright system
4. House of Burgesses
5. Opechancanough
6. Maryland's "Act Concerning Religion"

7. Sir William Berkeley
8. Barbados
9. Scrooby congregation
10. William Bradford
11. John Winthrop
12. Fundamental Orders of Connecticut
13. Thomas Hooker
14. Roger Williams
15. King Philip's War
16. Society of Friends
17. James Oglethorpe
18. Georgia Trustees
19. Edmund Andros
20. William and Mary
21. Jacob Leisler
22. John Coode

DOCUMENT

An expedition under Captain Christopher Newport began the Jamestown settlement in May 1607. In June, Captain Newport sailed for England, leaving behind 104 settlers. In September, only 46 of them were still living. One of the survivors, George Percy, wrote an account of the terrible time at Jamestown.

There were never Englishmen left in a foreign country in such misery as we were in this new discovered Virginia. We watched every three nights, lying on the bare cold ground, what weather soever came; and warded all the next day; which brought our men to be most feeble wretches. Our food was but a small can of barley, sodden in water, to five men a day. Our drink, cold water taken out of the river; which was at flood very salt; at low tide full of slime and filth, which was the destruction of many of our men. Thus we lived for the space of five months [from August 1607 to January 1608] in this miserable distress, not having five able men to man our bulwarks upon any occasion. If it had not pleased God to put a terror in the savages' hearts we had all perished by those wild and cruel pagans, being in that weak estate as we were; our men night and day groaning in every corner of the fort most pitiful to hear. . . . It pleased God after a while to send those people which were our mortal enemies; to relieve us with victuals, as breed, corn, fish, and flesh in great plenty, which was the setting up of our feeble men; otherwise we had all perished.

MAP EXERCISE

Fill in or identify the following on the blank map provided. Use the map on page 39 of the text as your source.

1. Colonial grants to Massachusetts Bay, Plymouth, New Haven, Hartford, Rhode Island, and the Duke of York.
2. Connecticut, New York, New Hampshire, and Maine.
3. Principal settlements in these colonies and the dates they were founded.
4. Connecticut River and the Merrimack River.
5. Lake Champlain, Massachusetts Bay, Cape Cod, Narragansett Bay, and the main islands along the coast.
6. The Mason and Gorges grants.

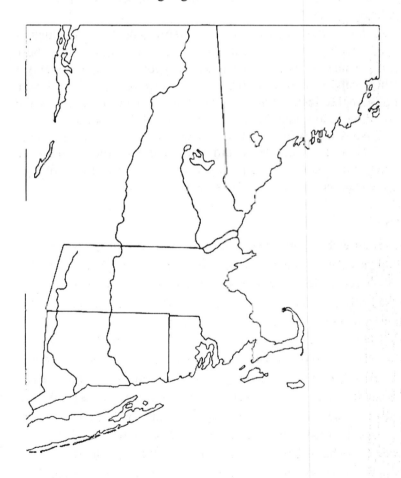

Interpretative Questions

Based on what you have filled in, answer the following. For some of the questions you will need to consult the narrative in your text for information or explanation.

1. Note the patterns of settlement in New England. What geographic features contributed to the placement of these early settlements? Why did these geographic features make a difference to early settlers?
2. Looking again at a physical map of the United States, determine which settlements were in the coastal plain, which were in the piedmont, and which were along the fall line. How did the location of these settlements influence their economic growth? How did location and subsequent economic growth shape the sort of societies that developed there?
3. Note the dates these settlements were established. What conclusions about the evolution of the settlements can you draw from these dates? (Consider political events as well as geographic conditions.)
4. Note the location of Boston, Providence, Hartford, and New Haven. What geographic features helped determine their locations? How did these features help shape the local economies of these settlements?
5. Massachusetts Bay was, or at least attempted to be, the dominant force in New England. How did that colony's land claims and expansion contribute to this? How did the location of new colonies serve to check the influence of Massachusetts Bay?

SUMMARY

During the seventeenth century, colonies were established in British North America, and the colonists began to perceive themselves as a hybrid breed. Before 1660, most colonies began as private ventures (with charters from the king), but the motives that brought them into being were as varied as the sociopolitical systems they developed. After 1660, proprietary colonies became the norm, and charters indicated a closer tie between the "owners" of a colony and the king, who granted the charter. As a result of this colonization effort, by the 1680s England had an unbroken string of provinces stretching from Canada to the Savannah River, as well as a number of island provinces in the Caribbean. As the colonies matured, their inhabitants began to exhibit an interest in exercising control over local affairs and an independence of interests that eventually led to trouble and confusion on both sides of the Atlantic. The problem was that at the very time that the colonists were developing distinctly

American attitudes and institutions, England, fully aware of the potential of its colonies, began to tighten control over its possessions.

CHAPTER SELF-TEST

After you have read the chapter in the text and done the exercises in the study guide, the following self-test can be taken to see if you understand the material you have covered. Answers appear at the end of the study guide.

Multiple Choice

Circle the letter of the response that best answers the question or completes the statement.

1. Which of the following did *not* shape the character of English settlements in America?
   a. The colonies were business enterprises.
   b. The colonies promoted freedom of religion.
   c. The colonies were designed to transplant society from the Old World to the New.
   d. The colonies were able to develop their own political and social institutions.

2. The year 1619 was important in the history of Virginia because that year the colony:
   a. elected its first House of Burgesses.
   b. made its first profit.
   c. received its first royal governor.
   d. put down an Indian uprising.

3. In 1616, two new elements were introduced into the Virginia social order. They were:
   a. women and Catholics.
   b. *mestizos* and blacks.
   c. blacks and women.
   d. women and *mestizos*.

4. In the end, Jamestown's survival was largely a result of :
   a. supplies sent from England.
   b. agricultural technologies developed by the Indians and borrowed by the English.
   c. the adaptation of Oriental farming practices.
   d. the ease with which European farming practices were adapted to the New World.

5. Which of the following colonies allowed freedom of religion to all Christians?
   a. Massachusetts
   b. Virginia
   c. Plymouth
   d. Maryland

6. Bacon's Rebellion was significant because:
   a. it revealed the bitterness of competition among rival elites in Virginia.
   b. it was evidence of the continuing struggle to define the Indian and white spheres of influence in Virginia.
   c. it demonstrated the potential for instability in the colony's large population of landless men.
   d. a and c
   e. All of the above.

7. Many Virginians turned to slaves rather than indentured servants for labor because Africans:
   a. already knew how to raise tobacco.
   b. did not have to be released, so there was no fear that they might become an unstable, landless class.
   c. were cheaper to purchase at the outset.
   d. were more naturally subservient and caused the master no trouble.

8. In the Caribbean planters turned to slave labor because:
   a. slaves already knew how to raise rice.
   b. slavery tended to make the society and culture more stable.
   c. sugar cultivation required a great deal of labor, which the native population could not supply.
   d. slaves could be kept for a long period of time and remain valuable.

9. The majority of colonists who first settled in Plymouth were:
   a. members of a Puritan Separatist congregation.
   b. not members of a Puritan Separatist congregation.
   c. upper-middle-class Puritans from the London area.
   d. moderate Puritans who wanted only minor reforms in church practices.

10. The first governor of the Massachusetts Bay colony was:
    a. John Winthrop.
    b. William Bradford.
    c. Roger Williams.
    d. Thomas Hooker.

11. Anne Hutchinson's teaching threatened to undermine the spiritual authority of the established clergy because she:
    a. claimed believers could communicate directly with God.
    b. preached that the clergy was corrupt.
    c. denounced clergymen who were also politicians.
    d. stressed faith over good works.

12. How was the fighting in King Philip's War and the Pequot War affected by earlier exchanges of technology between the English and the tribes?
    a. The English were able to use Indian weapons in close combat.
    b. The Indians used superior English knives and swords instead of stone age clubs.
    c. The English used cap and ball muskets.
    d. The Indians used the new flintlock muskets.

13. Slavery in Carolina was greatly influenced by slavery in:
    a. Virginia.
    b. Barbados.
    c. St. Augustine.
    d. England.

14. The Navigation Acts were designed to:
    a. regulate commerce according to the theory of mercantilism.
    b. destroy the power of rising colonial merchants.
    c. keep the price of tobacco low.
    d. raise money to pay off England's war debts.

15. The overthrow of James II in the Glorious Revolution was:
    a. well received in New England.
    b. criticized by colonial merchants.
    c. the result of pressure on Edmund Andros.
    d. hardly felt by colonial politicians.

True/False

Read each statement carefully. Mark true statements "T" and false statements "F."

___1. Virginia was a profitable colony from the start.
___2. The "headright" system was used to attract colonists to Virginia.
___3. Of the more than 8,500 settlers who came during Virginia's first seventeen years, more than 80 percent either abandoned the colony or died.
___4. Bacon's Rebellion successfully overthrew the government of Sir William Berkeley.

___5. The population of the English Caribbean colonies was equally divided between whites and blacks, freemen and slaves.

___6. The first enduring European settlement in New England was at Scrooby.

___7. Roger Williams insisted that the land on which Massachusetts was settled belonged to the Indians, not to the king.

___8. After New Englanders defeated the local Indians, the French refused to aid the Native Americans.

___9. John Locke was the author of the Fundamental Constitution for Carolina.

___10. When the English took New Amsterdam, they were able to quickly rid the colony of Dutch influences.

___11. Soon after Pennsylvania was founded, the Quakers became its largest religious group.

___12. The majority of colonists who came to Georgia were taken from debtors prison.

___13. New Englanders liked the idea of centralized authority under the Dominion of New England.

___14. The Navigation Acts increased the authority of the crown and decreased that of local governments.

___15. The colony that the crown could usually count on to support its policies was Massachusetts.

___16. As a result of the Glorious Revolution, religious toleration in Maryland continued.

Review Questions

These questions are to be answered with essays. This will allow you to explore relationships among individuals, events, and attitudes of the period under review.

1. Compare and contrast Virginia and Plymouth—their origins, their goals, and their early social, political, and economic development.
2. Between 1660 and 1700, the American colonies were shaken by a series of "revolts" that, it has been contended, were the result of tensions in colonial society. Examine the protests that took place in Virginia, Maryland, Massachusetts, and New York, and then compare and contrast the internal divisions that helped spark the outbreaks.
3. Explain the way in which England applied the principles of mercantilism to its North American colonies.
4. Compare and contrast the institution of slavery in England's mainland colonies with the institution as it existed in the Caribbean.

5. Compare and contrast the way the English and Spanish dealt with Native Americans. How were the goals of these Europeans both similar and different? How did the Native Americans respond to these Europeans? How were the outcomes of English and Spanish policies both similar and different? (Be sure to use material from this and the previous chapter in answering the question.)

CHAPTER THREE

Society and Culture in Provincial America

OBJECTIVES

A thorough study of Chapter 3 should enable you to understand:

1. The disagreement among historians concerning the origins of slavery.
2. The sources of colonial labor, including indentured servants, women, and imported Africans.
3. Immigration patterns and their effect on colonial development.
4. The ways in which factors of soil and climate determined the commercial and agricultural development of the colonies, despite crown attempts to influence production.
5. The emergence of the plantation system, and its impact on southern society.
6. How the increasing division of American societies by class spurred the growth of eighteenth-century consumerism.
7. The New England witchcraft episode as a reflection of Puritan society.
8. The reasons for the appearance of a variety of religious sects in the colonies, and the effect of the Great Awakening on the colonists.
9. The beginnings of colonial industry and commerce, and the early attempts at regulation by Parliament.
10. The ways in which colonial literature, education, science, law, and justice were diverging from their English antecedents.

PERTINENT QUESTIONS

The Colonial Population (pp. 60–69)

1. Explain the system of indentured servitude that developed in the American colonies.

2. What impact did freed indentures have on colonial sociopolitical development?
3. What factors contributed to the rapid increase in colonial population during the last half of the seventeenth century?
4. How did the importance of reproduction in the labor-scarce society of colonial America affect the status and lifecycle of women?
5. How and why did the status of women in colonial America differ from region to region?
6. Describe the steps that led to the establishment of black slavery in the English American colonies.
7. Why is 1697 considered a "turning point in the history of the black population in America"? What had this change resulted in by 1760?
8. What were the major non-English groups to migrate to America, and why did they come?
9. What were the general characteristics of the colonial population in the first half of the eighteenth century—its rate of growth, cultural composition, and settlement patterns?
10. Explain the debate among historians over how and why white Americans created a system of slave labor using African Americans.

The Colonial Economies (pp. 69–79)

11. Describe the economy of the Chesapeake region, and explain why it developed as it did.
12. How did the economies of South Carolina and Georgia differ from that of the Chesapeake? How were they similar?
13. Why did the northern colonies turn to economic pursuits other than agriculture? What obstacles did these new pursuits have to overcome?
14. What factors gave rise to colonial commercial enterprises? What obstacles did these enterprises have to overcome and what effect did their success have on the colonial economy?
15. What was the "triangular trade," and what does it reveal about colonial economics?
16. How did the increasing division of American societies by class spur the growth of eighteenth-century consumerism?

Patterns of Society (pp. 74–79)

17. How did the plantation system in the American South illustrate both the differences between the colonial and English class systems and the way in which colonial communities evolved in response to local conditions?
18. What were the characteristics of plantation slavery?

19. What were the characteristics of communities that emerged in Puritan New England?
20. How was the family central to the Puritan community?
21. How did the experience of America affect the patriarchal family?
22. What caused the witchcraft hysteria of the 1680s and 1690s, and what did these incidents reveal about the nature of Massachusetts society?
23. What forces gave rise to colonial "cities"?
24. Describe urban life in colonial America.

Awakenings and Enlightenments *(pp. 79–86)*

25. What were the major religious groups in the colonies, what elements formed them, and where were they located?
26. What was the Great Awakening? Who brought it about, and what groups supported or opposed it?
27. What were the effects of the Great Awakening?
28. What colonial colleges were in operation by 1763? Why was each founded, and what subjects were studied in the mid-eighteenth century?
29. Explain why science and technology were so important in colonial America.
30. Explain the working of the law in colonial America—the concepts on which it was based and the way it functioned.

IDENTIFICATION

Identify each of the following, and explain why it is important within the context of the chapter.

1. middle passage
2. Royal African Company
3. "slave codes"
4. Scotch-Irish
5. the Enlightenment
6. Peter Hasenclever
7. Stono Rebellion
8. town meeting
9. "visible saints"
10. "jeremiads"
11. George Whitefield
12. Jonathan Edwards
13. New Lights/Old Lights

14. "dame schools"
15. John Peter Zenger

DOCUMENT

Below is the report of the "confession" of Mary Osgood of Andover, Massachusetts, which was given on September 8, 1692, before a group of judges.

> She confesses that, about 11 years ago, when she was a melancholy state and condition, she used to walk abroad in her orchard; and upon a certain time she saw the appearance of a cat, at the end of the house, which yet she thought was a real cat. However, at that time, it diverted her from praying to God, and instead thereof she prayed to the devil; about which time she made a covenant with the devil, who, as a black man, came to her and presented her a book, upon which she laid her finger, and that left a red spot: and that upon her signing the devil told her he was God, and that she should serve and worship him, and she believes she consented to it. She says, further, that about two years agone, she was carried through the air, in company with deacon Frye's wife, Ebenezer Baker's wife, and Goody Tyler, to five mile pond, where she was baptised by the devil, who dipped her face in the water and made her renounce her former baptism, and told her she must be his, soul and body, forever, and that she must serve him, which she promised to do.

Six weeks later, Mrs. Osgood visited the Puritan divine Increase Mather. He reported that she had recanted.

> Mrs. Osgood freely and relentingly said that the confession which she made upon her examination for witchcraft, and afterwards acknowledged before the honourable judges, was wholly false, and that she was brought to the said confession by the violent urging and unreasonable pressings that were used toward her; she asserted that she never signed the devil's book, was never baptised by the devil, never afflicted any of the accusers, or gave her consent for their being afflicted.

In the light of what you have read in your text, what do these documents tell you about religion in the Massachusetts Bay colony, the relationship between church and state in that colony, and the impact of religion on the lives of the Puritans?

MAP EXERCISE

Fill in or identify the following on the blank map provided. Use the map on page 68 of the text as your source.

1. British North American colonies.
2. Colonial groups—Southern, Middle, and New England.
3. Principal settlements in each colony.
4. Principal rivers in each colony.
5. Using different colors, identify the dominant immigrant groups.

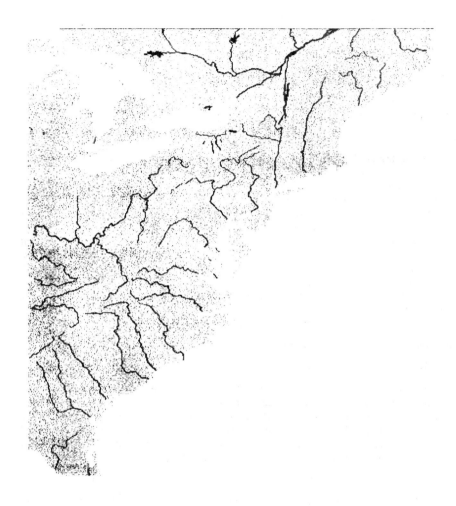

Interpretative Questions

Based on what you have filled in, answer the following. For some of the questions you will need to consult the narrative in your text for information or explanation.

1. What was the major non-English immigrant group in the southern colonies? What circumstances led to their immigration to the New World? Why were they concentrated in the South rather than in other regions?
2. Who were the Scotch-Irish? Why did they leave their homeland, and why did they settle where they did? How would the conditions that led to their immigration and settlement have affected their attitude toward England and English colonial governments.
3. Note the location of German immigrant groups. Why did they leave their homeland, and why did they settle where they did? How would the conditions that led to their immigration and settlement have affected their attitude toward England and English colonial governments?
4. Note where the English are concentrated. Which are the most "English" colonies and regions? Why would the southern colonies continue to have a strong English orientation despite the presence of a large immigrant group?

SUMMARY

After the turmoil of the late seventeenth century had subsided, it became evident that the English-American colonies and the colonists who populated them were beginning to develop characteristics that were distinctly "American." Although still essentially transplanted English subjects and still greatly influenced by European ideas and institutions, the colonists were also diverse, aggressive, and as concerned with their own success as with that of the empire of which they were part. New sources of wealth and new patterns of trade shaped the growth of the colonies, and new immigrants, not always from England, added a dimension unknown in the mother country. Although differences in geography, economy, and population gave each colony its own particular character and problems, there remained many common concerns—not the least of which was how to deal with, or avoid dealing with, British mercantile restrictions. In short, between 1700 and 1750, Britain's American colonies began to show signs of being both English and American; they were indeed "different," and it is this difference that Chapter 3 explores.

CHAPTER SELF-TEST

After you have read the chapter in the text and done the exercises in the study guide, the following self-test can be taken to see if you understand the material you have covered. Answers appear at the end of the study guide.

Multiple Choice

Circle the letter of the response that best answers the question or completes the statement.

1. During the seventeenth century, at least three-fourths of the immigrants who came to the Chesapeake colonies came as:
   a. slaves.
   b. artisans.
   c. indentured servants.
   d. convicts.

2. The biggest beneficiaries of the easy access into the field of medicine during the colonial era were:
   a. newly arrived immigrants.
   b. established physicians who could not get qualified assistants.
   c. women who became midwives.
   d. free blacks who used folk medicine.

3. Which of the following is true of gender relations in the colonies?
   a. Women married late and many did not marry at all.
   b. Women usually lived to see most of their children into maturity.
   c. The average wife experienced pregnancies every two years.
   d. There was little premarital sex in the colonies and few children were born out of wedlock.

4. The year 1697 marked a turning point in the history of the black population in America because:
   a. planters from Barbados came to Carolina.
   b. slavery was introduced in Georgia.
   c. Massachusetts and Rhode Island abolished slavery.
   d. the Royal Africa Company lost its monopoly.

5. The one factor which determined whether a person was subject to the slave codes in the British American colonies was:
   a. their country of origin.
   b. the ancestry of their father.
   c. the ancestry of their mother.
   d. their African ancestry.

6. The most numerous of the non-English immigrants were the:
   a. Scotch-Irish.
   b. Pennsylvania Dutch.
   c. French Huguenots.
   d. Scottish Highlanders.

7. Which of the following was *not* one of the biggest obstacles to industrialization in the British American colonies?
   a. Regulatory acts passed by Parliament
   b. An inadequate labor supply
   c. A small domestic market
   d. An inadequate transportation system

8. A common problem in American commerce in the seventeenth century was:
   a. the lack of a commonly accepted currency.
   b. an insufficient number of ships to carry colonial goods.
   c. the large number of big companies in every colony.
   d. a small, unprofitable coastal trade.

9. The maze of highly diverse trade routes that involved the buying and selling of rum, slaves, and sugar was known as the:
   a. staple system.
   b. triangular trade.
   c. middle passage.
   d. Atlantic highway.

10. During the seventeenth century, colonial plantations were:
    a. rough and relatively small.
    b. English country estates on a smaller scale.
    c. seats of an entrenched, landholding aristocracy.
    d. insignificant in the colonial economy.

11. The characteristic social unit in New England was the:
    a. isolated farm.
    b. meeting house.
    c. town.
    d. plantation.

12. Which of the following was *not* a function of a colonial American city?
    a. They were trading centers.
    b. They were centers of industry.
    c. They were intellectual centers.
    d. They were areas of few social distinctions.

13. In matters of religion, Americans were:
    a. less tolerant than their English counterparts.
    b. more tolerant than their English counterparts.
    c. more inclined to be members of an Anglican congregation.
    d. unconcerned about piety, especially in New England.

14. The Great Awakening was:
    a. an effort to alert colonists to British efforts to control them politically.
    b. the way the Enlightenment influenced American education.
    c. the opening of new commercial opportunities in the West.
    d. the first great American religious revival.

15. During the first half of the eighteenth century colonial legislatures were generally:
    a. able to act independently of Parliament.
    b. controlled by the governor.
    c. free from class distinctions.
    d. a reflection of democracy in their respective colonies.

True/False

Read each statement carefully. Mark true statements "T" and false statements "F."

___1.   After the 1650s natural increase became the most important source of population growth in New England.

___2.   The survival rate for children was higher in the South than in any other section.

___3.   The "middle passage" was the route taken by settlers trying to get to the Ohio Valley.

___4.   Africans were enslaved from the time of their arrival.

___5.   Between 1700 and 1775 the colonial population increased from under 300,000 to over 2 million.

___6.   Tobacco was the major cash crop in Georgia and South Carolina.

___7.   Industries that exploit natural resources are known as extractive industries.

___8. A great landowner in colonial America was powerful on his estate, but generally had no influence beyond the boundary of his property.

___9. There were no significant slave rebellions during the colonial era.

___10. The rigid patriarchal structure of the Puritan family limited opportunities for younger male members to strike out on their own.

___11. What happened during the witch trials at Salem was not repeated in other parts of New England.

___12. The outstanding preacher of the Great Awakening was Jonathan Edwards.

___13. With access to "dame schools," American women were able to enjoy a higher degree of literacy than men.

___14. Most of the early colleges in America were started for religious reasons.

___15. In the John Peter Zenger case, the court held that criticism of the government was not libelous if factually true.

Review Questions

These questions are to be answered with essays. This will allow you to explore relationships among individuals, events, and attitudes of the period under review.

1. Compare and contrast the economy of the northern colonies with that of the southern colonies. What made the two regions develop as they did? How did these economic systems reflect social systems emerging at the same time?

2. Write an essay in which you describe the diverse population that settled the British colonies in the sixteenth and seventeenth centuries, and assess its growth during this period.

3. By violating the Navigation Acts and developing their own trading patterns, were the American colonies creating their own mercantile system? Discuss this question and its implications for future relations between the colonies and England.

4. What role did religion play in the advance of education in America? In what way did religion also hinder education? After assessing these two relationships, show the extent to which the fruits of education (reading, writing, science, and law) flourished in America; at the same time, show how these helped to form a character that was "American."

5. What impact did technology have on the development of the British American colonies? (Be sure to use material from this and the previous chapter in answering this question.)

CHAPTER FOUR

The Empire Under Strain

OBJECTIVES

A thorough study of Chapter 4 should enable you to understand:

1. The primary reasons for the growth of the differences between colonial Americans and the British government that resulted in a clash of interests.
2. The colonial attitudes toward England and toward other colonies before the Great War for the Empire.
3. The causes of the Great War for the Empire, and the reasons for the French defeat.
4. The effects of the war on American colonists and on the status of the colonies within the British Empire.
5. The options for dealing with the colonies available to the British in 1763, and the reasons for adopting the policies that they chose to implement.
6. The importance of the series of crises from the Sugar Act through the Coercive Acts, and how each crisis changed colonial attitudes toward the mother country.
7. The change in American attitudes toward Parliament, the English constitution, and the king.
8. What slogans such as "No taxation without representation" really meant.
9. The significance of the convening of the First Continental Congress, and what it accomplished.

PERTINENT QUESTIONS

Loosening Ties (pp. 91–92)

1. How did the relationship between king and Parliament change during the early eighteenth century? What role did the prime minister play in this change?
2. How were the American colonies administered by Britain, from Britain, during this period? What was the effect of this policy?

3. How was England's hold on the colonies weakened between 1700 and 1775? What role did colonial assemblies play in this weakening?
4. What factors helped promote colonial unity during this period?
5. What was the Albany Plan, and what did it reveal about colonial unity?

The Struggle for the Continent (pp. 93–97)

6. To what areas of North America had the French laid claim by 1750?
7. What were the causes and results of Anglo-French conflicts between 1686 and 1748? What role did the American colonies of each play in these conflicts?
8. What caused the Great War for the Empire, and why is it called by that name?
9. How did the Great War for the Empire become a "global war," and how did Britain carry out its part in the struggle?
10. What role did the French and British colonies play in this war?
11. What were the terms of the Treaty of Paris of 1763?

The New Imperialism (pp. 97–101)

12. What dilemma faced London policymakers at the end of the Great War for the Empire?
13. What initial policy changes occurred when George III ascended the throne, and what were the king's motives in making these changes?
14. How were the policy changes cited in question 13 reflected in the acts passed under the Grenville administration? Deal with the specific acts as well as general policy objectives.
15. What was it about post-1763 British policy that would cause colonists in every section to see the disadvantages rather than the advantages of being part of the British Empire?

Stirrings of Revolt (pp. 101–109)

16. Why did the Stamp Act so antagonize the American colonists?
17. Who led the protests in Virginia over the Stamp Act? What reasons, other than those stated in the resolutions proposed, contributed to this action? What was the effect of the protests, and what were the results?
18. What was England's response to the American protests over the Stamp Act? How did the action by Townshend attempt to anticipate American attacks on future acts?
19. How did the policies of Lord North differ from those of his predecessors? In what ways were they alike?

20. What role did Samuel Adams play in the American protests? How did his view of the need for American independence differ from those of most other colonial leaders at the time?
21. How did the colonial view of the nature of the British Empire differ from the view by George III and his supporters?
22. What were the theories of government advanced by John Locke, and how did the American colonists apply them to their struggle with England?
23. How was tavern culture critical to the growth of Revolutionary sentiment in the colonies?
24. Why was the Tea Act seen by many Americans as a threat to themselves and their institutions?
25. What were the Coercive Acts? How did the Quebec Act help to unite the colonies with Boston, in opposition to these acts?

Cooperation and War (pp. 109–112)

26. What role was played by committees of correspondence in the American protests?
27. What were the five major decisions made at the First Continental Congress, and what was their significance?
28. What were the circumstances that led to the fighting at Lexington and Concord?

IDENTIFICATION

Identify each of the following, and explain why it is important within the context of the chapter.

1. Treaty of Utrecht
2. King George's War
3. William Pitt
4. James Wolfe
5. Proclamation of 1763
6. Sugar Act of 1764
7. Paxton Boys
8. Regulators
9. Sons of Liberty
10. Declaratory Act
11. committees of correspondence
12. Boston Massacre
13. "internal"/"external" taxes
14. "virtual" representation

15. Intolerable Acts
16. Continental Association

DOCUMENT

Below is an extract from the resolutions of the Stamp Act Congress, passed in
1765. Note the line of argument. How do the resolutions reflect attitudes toward
local control of local affairs developed over the preceding century?

I. That His Majesty's subjects in these colonies owe the same allegiance to the Crown
of Great Britain that is owing from his subjects born within the realm, and all due
subordination to that august body the Parliament of Great Britain.

II. That His Majesty's liege subjects in these colonies are entitled to all the inherent
rights and liberties of his natural born subjects within the kingdom of Great Britain.

III. That it is inseparably essential to the freedom of a people, and the undoubted right
of Englishmen, that no taxes be imposed on them but with their own consent, given
personally or by their representatives.

IV. That the people of these colonies are not, and from their local circumstances
cannot be, represented in the House of Commons in Great Britain.

V. That the only representatives of the people of these colonies are persons chosen
therein by themselves, and that no taxes ever have been, or can be constitutionally
imposed on them, but by their respective legislatures. . . .

MAP EXERCISE

Fill in or identify the following on the blank map provided. Use the map on page
98 of the text as your source.

1. Britain's North American colonies.
2. Other territory claimed by Britain.
3. Spanish claims.
4. Provincial capitals (British and Spanish).
5. Other principal colonial towns.
6. Non-Indian settlement before 1700.
7. Non-Indian settlement between 1700 and 1763.
8. Frontier line in 1763.
9. Proclamation Line of 1763.
10. Principal rivers, the Great Lakes, and the Appalachian Mountains.

Interpretative Questions

Based on what you have filled in, answer the following. For some of the
questions you will need to consult the narrative in your text for information or
explanation.

1. Note the frontier line in 1763 and consider how much territory east
   of this line had been settled. How would this settlement pattern
   support Britain's post-1763 policy concerning western expansion?
2. How does the Proclamation Line of 1763 correspond to the frontier
   line? Which areas would have been immediately affected by the
   line?

3. If settlement west of the Appalachian Mountains was restricted, where would the expanding population go? Which colonies might have actually benefited from the Proclamation Line? Explain.
4. Which colonies would be most negatively affected by the Proclamation Line of 1763? Explain.
5. From the names and locations of the settlements west of the Proclamation Line of 1763, do you think they would hinder or help the British accomplish their policy objectives in that region? Explain.

SUMMARY

Despite a number of disagreements, by 1763 Anglo-American ties seemed stronger than ever. The colonies had prospered under British rule, had developed local institutions through which they seemed to govern themselves, and finally, with the defeat of France, appeared ready to expand into the heart of the continent. However, no sooner was the war ended than the British began to alter the pre-1763 system in an effort to make it more efficient and more responsive to control from London. The means chosen to do this (enforced regulations to end the illegal trade that had flourished under salutary neglect, plus taxation to pay for the colonial administration) were seen in the colonies as threats to the way of life they had come to accept as rightfully theirs. Rising in protest, the colonies faced a British government determined to assert its authority, and, with neither side willing to give in, the cycle of action and reaction continued. Finally, spurred on by a propaganda campaign that characterized the mother country as a tyrant determined to bring America to its knees, the colonies acted. The Intolerable Acts proved the final straw, and in September 1774, twelve British provinces met in a Continental Congress in hopes that a united front would cause London to reconsider and that conflict would be avoided. But it did not work, and in the spring, fighting occurred at Lexington and Concord. Although independence was not yet declared, the American Revolution had begun.

CHAPTER SELF-TEST

After you have read the chapter in the text and done the exercises in the study guide, the following self-test can be taken to see if you understand the material you have covered. Answers appear at the end of the study guide.

Multiple Choice

Circle the letter of the response that best answers the question or completes the statement.

1. By the 1750s, colonial legislatures had come to see themselves as:
   a. little Parliaments.
   b. agents of the royal governor.
   c. powerless.
   d. agents for democratic reform.

2. The British victory in the Great War for the Empire:
   a. expelled France and Spain from North America.
   b. gave England control of North America east of the Mississippi River.
   c. resulted in the defeat of all North American Indian tribes.
   d. resulted in less contact between British authority and American colonists.

3. Prior to the Great War for the Empire, the Iroquois Confederacy:
   a. traded exclusively with the English.
   b. traded exclusively with the French.
   c. maintained their autonomy by avoiding a close relationship with both the French and the English.
   d. traded only with the five tribes that made up the Confederacy.

4. Which of the following did *not* occur during the Great War for the Empire?
   a. Americans were reimbursed for supplies requisitioned in their British colonies.
   b. Colonial assemblies were in charge of recruitment in their respective colonies.
   c. The French lost the city of Quebec.
   d. Most of the fighting was done by colonial militia.

5. The result of the Great War for the Empire was a disaster for:
   a. English frontiersmen and traders.
   b. colonial merchants.
   c. the Iroquois Confederacy.
   d. the Royal Africa Company.

6. The English decision to reorganize the British Empire after 1763 was the result of:
   a. colonial demands for more efficient government.
   b. problems in the merchant community and their desire for regulation.
   c. colonial unrest, which the British government planned to put down before it became serious.
   d. a need to administer an empire that was now twice as large as it had been.

7. In an effort to keep peace between frontiersmen and Indians, and to provide for a more orderly settlement of the West, the British government:
   a. forbade settlers from crossing the mountains that divided the Atlantic coast from the interior.
   b. gave Indian tribes and confederations colonial status.
   c. allowed interior settlement only if settlers bought land from the tribes.
   d. put forts in the Ohio Valley to protect settlers there.

8. Which of the following was a consequence of the policies of the Grenville ministry?
   a. British tax revenues in the colonies increased 10 times.
   b. Colonists effectively resisted and paid little tax.
   c. Many colonial merchants went out of business.
   d. Colonial assemblies assumed the responsibility for taxing their individual colonies.

9. British policies after 1763:
   a. destroyed the economy of the American colonies.
   b. stripped colonial assemblies of their authority.
   c. created a deep sense of economic unease, particularly in colonial cities.
   d. actually helped the colonial economy.

10. Colonists argued that the Stamp Act was not proper because:
    a. it affected only a few people, so the burden was not shared.
    b. the money raised would not be spent in the colonies.
    c. colonies could be taxed only by their provincial assemblies.
    d. the tax was too high.

11. Townshend believed his taxes on the colonists would not be protested because they were:
    a. "external" taxes—taxes on goods brought from overseas.
    b. not going to be strictly enforced.
    c. lower than the Stamp Act taxes.
    d. to be used to support colonial projects.

12. Colonial "committees of correspondence" were created to:
    a. keep colonial intellectuals in contact with each other.
    b. publicize grievances against England.
    c. improve the writing skills of young gentlemen.
    d. correspond with English radicals who supported the American cause.

13. Colonists felt that when the English constitution was allowed to function properly, it created the best political system because it:
    a. distributed power among the three elements of society—the monarchy, the aristocracy, and the common people.
    b. created a republican government.
    c. created a democracy.
    d. put power in the hands of those best suited to govern.

14. Tavern culture of the colonies was crucial to the growth of Revolutionary sentiment because:
    a. taverns were appealing because they provided alcoholic drinks.
    b. taverns were among the few public spaces where people could meet and talk openly.
    c. the tavern was a mostly male institution and politics were a male concern.
    d. All of the above

15. The Coercive Acts, or Intolerable Acts:
    a. isolated Massachusetts from the other colonies.
    b. made Massachusetts a martyr in the eyes of other colonists.
    c. created no concern among any group other than merchants.
    d. increased the power of colonial assemblies.

16. Which of the following was *not* a step taken by the First Continental Congress?
    a. It adopted a plan for a colonial union under British authority.
    b. It endorsed a statement of grievances.
    c. It called for military preparations.
    d. It called for a series of boycotts.

True/False

Read each statement carefully. Mark true statements "T" and false statements "F."

___1.   By the 1750s, most Americans felt little loyalty to the British crown.

___2.   The French were able to forge good relations with the Indian tribes because they were more tolerant of the Indian way of life than the British.

___3.   Before the Great War for the Empire, England, France, and Spain had been at peace with each other for nearly half a century.

___4.   The Seven Years War, the French and Indian War, and the Great War for the Empire are all the same war.

___5.   After the Peace of Paris of 1763, the English were inclined to let the colonies go their own way, with few restrictions.

___6.   England was fortunate that King George III was young, bright, and surprisingly mature for his age.

___7.   Because they needed protection, colonists in both the East and the West were glad to have regular British troops stationed permanently in America.

___8.   The formation of groups known as the "Paxton Boys" and the "Regulators" revealed that colonists in the West believed they were not being treated fairly by colonists in the East.

___9.   Colonists were concerned over the immediate impact of the Stamp Act, not its long-range implications.

___10. Parliament repealed the Stamp Act, and in the Declaratory Act it declared that it would not tax the colonies in this way again.

___11. Colonists responded to the Townshend Duties with agreements not to import the taxed goods.

___12. Americans wanted their representatives to "actually" represent them, while the British claimed that Parliament represented all British citizens, no matter where they lived.

___13. Women, especially southern women, took no part in the protests and boycotts rising from the Coercive Acts.

___14. Those who attended the Continental Congress did not intend for it to be a continuing organization.

___15. The fighting at Lexington and Concord caused many who previously had little enthusiasm for the rebel cause to rally to it.

Review Questions

These questions are to be answered with essays. This will allow you to explore relationships among individuals, events, and attitudes of the period under review.

1. Explain the role that colonial assemblies played in the American protests of British policies after 1763. Why did the assemblies take such a leading role, and what effect did the British attitude (and action) toward these legislatures have on the American decision to revolt?

2. It has been said that Americans revolted against tyranny anticipated, rather than against tyranny inflicted. Define tyranny as you believe an eighteenth-century American might have, and then assess this point of view.

3. From the outset, Massachusetts was the leader of the anti-British protest studied in this chapter. Why? What factors in the economic, political, and intellectual climate of that colony made it such a hotbed of revolution? What part did Puritanism play in shaping this climate? (Be sure to check previous chapters when preparing your answer.)

CHAPTER FIVE

The American Revolution

OBJECTIVES

A thorough study of Chapter 5 should enable you to understand:

1. American war aims, and the problems experienced by the Revolutionary governments in carrying on a protracted war.
2. The aim of the Declaration of Independence, the reasons for its issuance, and its influence throughout the world since 1776.
3. The indispensable contributions of George Washington to the successful outcome of the Revolution.
4. The diplomatic triumph for American negotiators embodied in the Treaty of Paris.
5. The features of the Articles of Confederation, and the reasons for its creation.
6. The problems faced by the government under the Articles of Confederation and how they were addressed.
7. How the modern idea of revolution was a product of the ideas of the Enlightenment.
8. The ways in which the American Revolution was in many ways the most influential of the Enlightenment-driven revolutions.

PERTINENT QUESTIONS

The States United (pp. 118–122)

1. List the divisions within the Second Continental Congress, and give the aim of each faction. How did they attempt to gain their ends?
2. How did the pamphlet *Common Sense* address the problem of the aim of the war, and what was its impact on American opinion?
3. What were the philosophical roots of the Declaration of Independence, and what effect did the Declaration have on the struggle?
4. What problems did the Americans face in providing the necessary supplies and equipment for the war and in paying for them?

5. What were the American advantages in the struggle, and why was George Washington selected as the best person to make the most of these advantages?

6. Identify and explain the two broad schools of interpretation that emerged as historians debated the origins of the American Revolution. On what points do these interpretations differ?

The War for Independence (pp. 122–129)

7. What were the initial setbacks in the war during 1776, and what was the significance of the Battles of Trenton and Princeton in this regard?

8. What was the initial plan for the British campaign of 1777? How was this altered, and what effect did this alteration have on the outcome?

9. What were the American diplomatic goals at the start of the war? What problems did they face, and what efforts were made to overcome them?

10. How did the victory at Saratoga affect American diplomatic efforts? How did England and France respond to this news? What was the result?

11. Why did the British decide to launch a campaign against the southern colonies in 1778? What advantages and disadvantages did each side have in this region?

12. How was the campaign in the South conducted, and why was the victory at Yorktown so significant for the Americans?

13. What were the provisions of the Treaty of Paris in 1783, and how did the treaty affect relations among the United States, France, and Spain?

14. What problems did the Treaty of Paris of 1783 fail to solve? What problems did it create?

War and Society (pp. 129–135)

15. Who were the Loyalists? What elements in America remained loyal to the king, and for what reasons?

16. What impact did the American Revolution have on Native Americans?

17. How did the Revolution affect the way American women thought about their status, and what changes resulted from this new awareness?

18. What changes did the Revolution produce in the structure of the American economy?

The Creation of State Governments (pp. 135–138)

19. What was it about the concept of a republican government that so appealed to Americans?
20. How did Americans propose to avoid what they considered to be the problems of the British system they were repudiating?
21. What were the characteristics of the state constitutions written during the early years of the struggle? How did they reflect the general spirit of the Enlightenment—the belief that freedom was the natural state of humanity?
22. What impact did the Revolution have on slavery in New England? In the middle states? In the South?

The Search for a National Government (pp. 138–143)

23. What type of government did the Articles of Confederation create? What were its major features?
24. How did the Treaty of Paris of 1783 fail to resolve, or in some cases help to create strain among the United States, England, and Spain?
25. What commercial arrangements did American shippers and traders want above all others after the war had ended? Why did they feel this was needed, and how successful were they in accomplishing their aims?
26. What effect did the American westward movement have on diplomatic relations with Great Britain and Spain?
27. How did the Confederation Congress attempt to solve the problem of the status of western territory the states had ceded to the national government? Which interest groups favored which plans for the sale and distribution of land?
28. What were the sources of the Confederation's postwar economic problems, and how did the government attempt to solve them? What were the results?
29. How was paper money seen as a solution to the economic problems of one element in American society? Who opposed this and why?
30. How did the action of Daniel Shays and his followers relate to the economic problem of the Confederation period? What was the significance of the movement he led?

IDENTIFICATION

Identify each of the following, and explain why it is important within the context of the chapter.

1. Benedict Arnold
2. Sir William Howe
3. John Burgoyne
4. Count de Vergennes
5. Sir Henry Clinton
6. Lord Cornwallis
7. Nathanael Greene
8. Thomas Jeremiah
9. Dragging Canoe
10. Judith Sargent Murray
11. Virginia Statute of Religious Liberty
12. Little Turtle
13. Ordinance of 1784
14. township
15. Northwest Ordinance
16. Treaty of Greenville
17. Robert Morris

DOCUMENT 1

Read the Declaration of Independence, reproduced in the Appendices to your text. This is a statement of the causes for the colonists' rebelling against England. How do these causes set down by Jefferson compare with those you have identified earlier in your reading?

The Declaration of Independence also suggests the type of society that Americans hoped would result from this struggle. Identify the major characteristics of the independent nation that Jefferson hoped would be created.

DOCUMENT 2

The following is an excerpt from the Articles of Confederation, approved by all the states by 1781. How does it reflect the principles for which Americans said they were fighting the Revolution? What goals and objectives of the Revolution still remained to be achieved?

1. [Article II] "Each state retains its sovereignty, freedom, and independence, and every Power, Jurisdiction and right, which is not by this confederation expressly delegated to the United States, in Congress assembled."

2. [Article IV] The free inhabitants of each state "shall be entitled to all privileges and immunities of free citizens in the several states" and "full faith and credit" shall be given by each state to the judicial and other official proceedings of other states.

3. [Article V] Each state shall be represented in Congress by no less than two and no more than seven members, shall pay its own delegates, and shall have one vote (regardless of the number of members).

4. [Article VI] No state, without the consent of Congress, shall enter into diplomatic relations or make treaties with other states or with foreign nations, or engage in war except in the case of actual invasion.

5. [Article VIII] A "common treasury" shall be supplied by the states in proportion to the value of their land and improvements; the states shall levy taxes to raise their quotas of revenue.

6. [Article IX] Congress shall have power to decide on peace and war, conduct foreign affairs, settle disputes between states, regulate the Indian trade, maintain post offices, make appropriations, borrow money, emit bills of credit, build a navy, requisition soldiers from the states, etc.—but nine states must agree before Congress can take any important action.

7. [Article X] A "Committee of the States," consisting of one delegate from each state, shall act in the place of Congress when Congress is not in session.

8. [Article XIII] No change shall be made in these articles unless agreed to by Congress and "afterwards confirmed by the legislatures of every state."

Summary

Between 1775 and 1787, Americans struggled to win a war, make a peace, and create ideologically sound, stable governments on both the state and the national levels. By the end of the era, there was little doubt that they had accomplished the first two of their goals, but serious questions were being raised concerning the success of the last. Despite problems that would have stopped lesser men, George Washington and his army had been able to successfully keep the British at bay, winning when they could and losing as seldom as possible. Meanwhile, the Continental Congress, blessed with some remarkable diplomats, maintained a foreign policy, the success of which can be seen in the Franco-American alliance of 1778 and the Treaty of Paris of 1783. But once the war ended, the government that the British threat had held together found that its member states' unwillingness to centralize power created more problems than it solved. Economic dislocation, exemplified by Daniel Shays and his followers, plagued the nation, as many thoughtful men searched for a way to transform Revolutionary rhetoric into reality and to restore order without sacrificing liberty.

CHAPTER SELF-TEST

After you have read the chapter in the text and done the exercises in the study guide, the following self-test can be taken to see if you understand the material you have covered. Answers appear at the end of the study guide.

Multiple Choice

Circle the letter of the response that best answers the question or completes the statement.

1. Thomas Paine's *Common Sense* is an important work because it:
   a. helped Americans reconcile their differences with England.
   b. persuaded Americans that no reconciliation with Britain was possible.
   c. supported the concept of the English constitution.
   d. argued that Parliament, not the king, was the enemy.

2. The Declaration of Independence stated that governments were formed to:
   a. give men an opportunity to exert power.
   b. reward loyal servants of the state.
   c. promote democracy.
   d. protect a person's life, freedom, and right to pursue happiness.

3. The longstanding debate over the origins of the American Revolution was mainly over whether or not:
   a. Revolutionaries really believed that *all* men were created equal.
   b. military men like Washington wanted war to advance their careers.
   c. it was a struggle for ideals and principles or a struggle for material gain.
   d. it was an effort by colonial elites to establish a monarchy or a movement of colonial radicals to establish a farmer's democracy.

4. Congress financed the Revolution by:
   a. selling bonds.
   b. minting gold and silver coins.
   c. borrowing from other nations.
   d. taxing the wealthy.

49

5. The choice of George Washington as commander in chief was a good one because of his:
   a. knowledge of military affairs.
   b. image among the people, who trusted and respected him.
   c. successful military experience in the Great War for the Empire.
   d. relaxed, informal way with his men.

6. At the end of 1776 the American army under Washington had:
   a. won no victories, major or minor.
   b. become badly divided and scattered.
   c. retreated into western Pennsylvania.
   d. won two minor victories and remained intact.

7. Which of the following was not part of the British strategy to cut the United States in two in 1777?
   a. Move forces up the Hudson from New York City.
   b. Prepare a two-pronged attack along the Mohawk and the upper Hudson.
   c. Capture Charleston.
   d. Bring an army down from Canada to meet the one coming up from New York.

8. John Burgoyne's surrender at Saratoga:
   a. convinced the French that they should help the Americans.
   b. caused the British to consider giving up the fight.
   c. made George Washington a military hero.
   d. had little effect on the war in the long run.

9. After 1777, the British decided to focus their efforts in the South because:
   a. there was less population there.
   b. they believed there were more Loyalists there.
   c. they thought slaves would help them.
   d. they had more Indian allies there.

10. The British were forced to surrender at Yorktown because:
    a. French troops and a French fleet helped trap the British.
    b. Washington was able to defeat the British in the field.
    c. Americans were better trained than the British.
    d. the British commander underestimated the size of Washington's army.

11. Even though the British wanted to end the war, the French were reluctant to negotiate because:
    a. they feared the Americans might take Canada.
    b. British agents were at work among the common folk of Paris.
    c. they were committed to staying in the war until Spain got Gibraltar.
    d. Spain was insisting on getting the Virgin Islands.

12. Of all the Loyalist groups in America, the one which suffered most as a result of the Revolution was:
    a. western farmers.
    b. slaves.
    c. traders and trappers.
    d. Anglicans.

13. During the Revolution women took on new responsibilities. After the war:
    a. things generally went back to the way they were before and few concrete reforms in the status of women occurred.
    b. women were able to translate wartime gains into peacetime reforms.
    c. women were recognized and honored for their contributions with new careers.
    d. women got the right to vote in most Northern colonies.

14. If postwar Americans agreed on nothing else, they agreed that:
    a. there should be no property qualifications to vote.
    b. states should have democratic governments.
    c. new governments should be republican.
    d. some men were born to govern and some were born to follow.

15. Under the Articles of Confederation, the only institution of national authority was the:
    a. Supreme Court.
    b. Congress.
    c. President of the United States.
    d. Senate.

True/False

Read each statement carefully. Mark true statements "T" and false statements "F."

___1.   When the fighting began, most Americans wanted the colonies to be independent from Great Britain.

___2. The rebelling colonies had access to sufficient local resources to fight a successful revolution.

___3. The British lacked the resources to conduct a war on the American continent.

___4. At the outset of the war, American leaders hoped that Canada would become the fourteenth state.

___5. The surrender of Burgoyne at Saratoga had no effect on the Iroquois Confederacy, since most of the Indians supported the American cause.

___6. There is no actual proof that Benedict Arnold committed treason.

___7. As a result of the Treaty of Paris of 1783, the new American nation's western boundary was the Blue Ridge Mountains.

___8. At least one-fifth, and maybe as many as one-third, of the American colonists were loyal to Britain during the Revolution.

___9. Native Americans were pleased with the outcome of the Revolution because it reduced the desire of colonists for western land.

___10. The first state constitutions written during the American Revolution generally reduced the power of the executive.

___11. In the newly created states, the privileges that churches enjoyed in the colonial era were largely stripped away.

___12. After independence, the United States quickly and easily persuaded Great Britain to abide by the terms of the treaty of 1783.

___13. The system for surveying and selling western lands set up under the Ordinance of 1785 favored small farmers.

___14. The Northwest Ordinance laid out the requirements for western territories to become states.

___15. During the period under consideration in this chapter, Congress did nothing to limit the expansion of slavery.

Review Questions

These questions are to be answered with essays. This will allow you to explore relationships among individuals, events, and attitudes of the period under review.

1. Explain how conflicts and rivalries among European nations both helped and hindered the American struggle for independence. (Be sure to consult previous chapters when answering this question.)

2. Compare and contrast the British and the American conduct of the war. How did each side propose to "win," how realistic was its

assessment of the situation, and how did this prewar assessment influence the ultimate outcome of the war?

3. Examine the relative successes and failures of the Articles of Confederation. Do you think that this government was capable of providing the stability that the new nation needed? Why or why not?

4. How did Revolutionary ideology challenge the way minorities were treated in America? What changes in this treatment resulted from this challenge, and why did some minorities find their circumstances improved while others did not?

5. Explain how the political ideology that was the foundation of the American Revolution influenced the writing of state constitutions and the Articles of Confederation. How did the colonial experience of the states help shape this political ideology? (Be sure to consult previous chapters when answering this question).

CHAPTER SIX

The Constitution and the New Republic

OBJECTIVES

A thorough study of Chapter 6 should enable you to understand:

1. The groups that advocated a stronger national government, and how they, probably a minority, were able to achieve their objective.
2. The origin of the Constitutional Convention, who the delegates were, how well they represented the people, and how well they were able to achieve a consensus.
3. Federalism and how the Constitution is designed to make it work.
4. The importance of *The Federalist Papers* in the ratification struggle, and their significance in years since.
5. The effectiveness of George Washington's solutions to the problems of the presidency, and how Washington, as its first occupant, affected the office and the nation.
6. The financial program of Alexander Hamilton, and its contribution to the success of the new government.
7. The ways in which the weak new nation coped with international problems, and the importance of such events as Washington's decision for neutrality and the "quasi war" with France.
8. The emergence of political parties, their political philosophies, and their influence through the election of 1800.

PERTINENT QUESTIONS

Framing a New Government (pp. 147–151)

1. Who were the advocates of centralization, and why did they want to alter or abolish the Articles of Confederation?
2. What did those who favored centralization see as the most serious problem of the Articles, and how would they have changed them? What had prevented these changes?

3. What were the characteristics of the men who met at the Constitutional Convention in Philadelphia? Whose presence was essential to the meeting's success? Why?
4. What were the two major points of view that divided the convention? What plans did each side propose to carry its view?
5. How were the differences between the "large state" and the "small state" plans resolved? What other issues divided the convention, and how were they resolved?
6. What was to be the role of various branches of government under the new Constitution?

Adoption and Adaptation (pp. 152–154)

7. Why did the supporters of the new Constitution call themselves "Federalists"? Were they actually Federalists, or did their philosophy of government reveal them to be something else? If so, what?
8. What method did the Federalists employ to get their views across to the people? What were their arguments, and how did the "Antifederalists" respond?
9. What was the process by which the Constitution was finally ratified? Which states supported it, by what margins, and which states did not? What objections were raised by the states?
10. What was the process by which the new government set up operations? What were the initial matters discussed, and how were they resolved?
11. In what way did Congress continue the work of the Constitutional Convention? What "gaps" in the Constitution did Congress fill?
12. Who were the men Washington selected for his cabinet, and on what basis did he choose them?

Federalists and Republicans (pp. 154–158)

13. How did the divisions of the 1790s reflect the differences in philosophy that were at the heart of the debate over the Constitution?
14. What was the view of society and politics held by Hamilton? Who did he feel should govern, and why?
15. What was Hamilton's plan for paying the nation's debts and restoring credit on a sound basis? To which social economic, and political groups would this have appealed?
16. How did Hamilton propose to enact his programs? Who opposed him, and to what degree was Hamilton successful?
17. How did political parties rise as a result of Hamilton's programs?
18. What was the political philosophy of Jefferson and Madison? How did it differ from that of Hamilton?

19. How did the French Revolution highlight the differences between the Federalists and the Republicans?

Establishing National Sovereignty (pp. 158–160)

20. How did Washington's reaction to the Whiskey Rebellion underscore the difference between the Constitution and the Articles of Confederation?
21. How did the government under the Constitution guarantee that people on the frontier would be loyal to it? What was the impact on Native Americans?
22. What diplomatic problem did the French Revolution and the war that followed pose for the United States? How did Washington and Congress deal with this problem?
23. What were the circumstances that sent John Jay to England, and what were the results of his mission?
24. How did Jay's Treaty affect American relations with Spain?

The Downfall of the Federalists (pp. 161–164)

25. Why was John Adams selected as the Federalist candidate in 1796?
26. What circumstances led to an administration with a Federalist president and a Republican vice president?
27. What caused the "quasi war" with France during the Adams administration? What was the result of this struggle?
28. How did the Federalists attempt to silence those who opposed the undeclared war, and what groups did these attempts most affect?
29. What gave rise to the Virginia and Kentucky Resolutions, and what attitude toward the nature of the federal government did these resolutions reveal?
30. What were the issues in the election of 1800, and what strategy did each party employ to get elected?
31. What was the outcome of the election of 1800, and what were the reactions of the losers and the victors?

IDENTIFICATION

Identify each of the following, and explain why it is important within the context of the chapter.

1. Annapolis Conference
2. Virginia Plan
3. New Jersey Plan
4. "Great Compromise"
5. Antifederalists

6. The Federalist Papers
7. Bill of Rights
8. Judiciary Act of 1789
9. XYZ Affair
10. Hamilton's bank bill
11. Hamilton's Report on Manufactures
12. Jay's Treaty
13. Pinckney's Treaty
14. Alien and Sedition Acts
15. Virginia and Kentucky Resolutions
16. Aaron Burr
17. Judiciary Act of 1801
18. "midnight appointments"

DOCUMENT

The document to be studied is the Constitution of the United States and its first twelve amendments. First, read the Constitution, in the Appendices to your text; then, consider the following.

1. How does the organization and election of the House and the Senate reflect attitudes that existed in 1787? Why is the impeachment held in the House and the trial in the Senate? What does this tell you about the Founding Fathers' attitude toward "popular" government?
2. Why are all revenue bills required to originate in the House of Representatives?
3. Examine the powers given Congress in Article I, Section 8. How does this section make the Constitution different from the Articles of Confederation?
4. Outline how the president was elected before the ratification of the Twelfth Amendment. What role did the popular vote play in this process? Why was it designed this way?
5. List the specific powers given the president, and be prepared to follow the evolution of these powers.
6. Why are Supreme Court justices (and judges on inferior courts) appointed rather than elected, and why do they "hold their offices during good behavior"? Look at the terms of office for the other branches. What does this reveal about what the people can and cannot do regarding changes in their government? Why was it done this way?

7. How does the amendment process under the Constitution differ from that under the Articles of Confederation? Why was this change made?

8. Reread the second paragraph of Article VI. According to this article, is the Constitution creating a national or a federal government?

Now read the first ten amendments to the Constitution—the Bill of Rights—and consider the following.

1. Look carefully at Amendments I and V, and consider the relations between Great Britain and its colonies from 1700 to 1776. It has been contended that these amendments were insisted on to make sure that the abuses experienced at the hands of the mother country would not be repeated. What evidence of this do you find?

2. Examine Amendments VI to VIII. What fears do these amendments reflect, and how were these fears resolved?

3. What seems to have been the purpose of Amendments IX and X? How do these amendments reflect concerns felt by opponents of the Constitution?

4. Compare and contrast the provisions in Amendment XII for electing the president with those in Article II, Section 1. What circumstances gave rise to this change?

MAP EXERCISE

Fill in or identify the following on the blank map provided. Use the maps in the text as your sources and consult maps in your library as needed.

1. Original thirteen states.
2. States admitted to the Union between the Revolution and 1800.
3. Ohio, Mississippi, Tennessee, and Missouri Rivers.
4. Territory held or claimed by Spain.
5. New Orleans, Mobile, and Pittsburgh.
6. The Appalachian Mountains.

Interpretative Questions

Based on what you have filled in, answer the following. For some of the
questions you will need to consult the narrative in your text for information or
explanation.

1. Thomas Jefferson "believed that farmers were God's chosen people
   and that an ideal republic would consist of sturdy citizens, each
   tilling his own soil." Furthermore, he advocated policies designed to
   make this republican ideal a reality. Which groups would have been
   most likely to support Jefferson because of this? Where were they
   located?

2. Which groups were most likely to oppose Jefferson? Where were
   they located? Why were members of this opposition less inclined to
   support the admission of new states?

3. Why did farmers in western Pennsylvania challenge federal authority
   in 1794? What did their location, and the nature of their economy
   have to do with this?

4. What Indian problems did the new nation experience? What role did the Spanish play in this? How were these problems solved?
5. Identify the settlements and area of the United States affected by Jay's Treaty. Why did some regions oppose this treaty?
6. Identify the areas of the United States affected by Pinckney's Treaty. How did this treaty solve (for the time being) one of the major problems facing western expansion?

SUMMARY

The period between 1785 and 1800 was one of the most politically productive in American history. During these fifteen years, the nation, guided by some of the most talented men in history, reorganized itself under a new framework of government and then struggled to define (for itself as well a for others) just what had been created. It was a period marked by the rise of a party that called itself Federalist, although the philosophy it espoused was, as its opponents were quick to point out, more "nationalist" in emphasis. Arguing that to prosper, the United States had best follow the economic and political example of Great Britain, these Federalists, led by Hamilton, interjected foreign policy into domestic differences and set the stage for one of the earliest and most serious assaults by the government on individual civil liberties. Seeing their less elitist, pro-agriculture Republican opponents as supporters of France in an undeclared conflict between that nation and the United States, the Federalists set out to suppress dissent and those who promoted it. This assault brought a swift response and so heightened tensions that many feared that the nation could not survive. It was against this background that a shift of power occurred, and by the end of the decade, the Federalists, who had been the moving force for so many years, were clearly losing ground to the Republicans. This meant that if wounds were to be healed and divisions mended, it would have to be done by the man many believed to be the personification of all that separated the two groups—Thomas Jefferson.

CHAPTER SELF-TEST

After you have read the chapter in the text and done the exercises in the study guide, the following self-test can be taken to see if you understand the material you have covered. Answers appear at the end of the study guide.

Multiple Choice

Circle the letter of the response that best answers the question or completes the statement.

1. By 1786, even defenders of the Articles of Confederation accepted the fact that it was necessary to strengthen:
   a. the power to tax.
   b. the executive.
   c. the court system.
   d. the army.

2. Which of the following was *not* a characteristic of the men who attended the Constitutional Convention in 1787?
   a. They represented the great property interests.
   b. They were relatively young.
   c. They believed in democracy.
   d. They were well educated.

3. The most significant division in the Constitutional Convention was between:
   a. slave and free states.
   b. large and small states.
   c. Eastern and Western interests.
   d. agricultural and manufacturing interests.

4. The most important issue left unaddressed when the Constitutional Convention adjourned was:
   a. the question of counting slaves for representation.
   b. whether to have an executive or not.
   c. the absence of a list of individual rights.
   d. the question of the power of the national government to tax.

5. The Constitution's most distinctive feature was its:
   a. "separation of powers" with "checks and balances."
   b. system for the direct election of the executive.
   c. lack of a national judicial system.
   d. single-house legislature.

6. Which of the following was *not* addressed by the first Congress under the new Constitution?
   a. A Bill of Rights.
   b. A federal court system.
   c. An executive department.
   d. The role of political parties in the election of a president.

7. Which of the following was *not* a belief of Alexander Hamilton?
   a. The best leaders are those democratically elected.
   b. A stable and effective government requires an elite ruling class.
   c. The new government needed the support of the wealthy and powerful.
   d. A permanent national debt was desirable.

8. Small farmers, who comprised the majority of the population, opposed Hamilton's plan on the grounds that it:
   a. taxed them excessively.
   b. favored a small, wealthy elite.
   c. created too many government offices.
   d. put power in the hands of slaveholders.
   e. a and b
   f. c and d

9. Jefferson and his followers believed the Federalists were creating a political party because they were:
   a. using their offices to reward supporters and win allies.
   b. forming local associations to strengthen their stand in local communities.
   c. working to establish a national network of influence.
   d. All of the above.

10. Which of the following was *not* a belief held by Jefferson and his followers?
    a. The ordinary farmer-citizen could, if properly educated, be trusted to govern through elected representatives.
    b. Urban people posed a danger to a republic, because they could easily become a lawless mob.
    c. The best citizen was one who tilled his own soil.
    d. Commercial activity was a danger to the republic.

11. Under the Constitution, the status of the western Indian tribes was:
    a. not clearly defined.
    b. that of independent nations.
    c. that of conquered nations.
    d. the same as states.

12. Although the treaty between England and the United States that John Jay negotiated in 1794 fell short of his instructions, it did:
    a. produce reasonably satisfactory commercial relations with England.
    b. give America undisputed sovereignty over Louisiana.
    c. end the impressment of American soldiers.
    d. indicate that the United States and France were not going to war with each other.

13. In the election of 1796:
    a. Thomas Jefferson was the choice of southern Federalists.
    b. the Federalist party united behind Hamilton.
    c. George Washington took an active role.
    d. without Washington to mediate, the Federalist party divided.

14. Republicans pinned their hopes for a reversal of the Alien and Sedition Acts on the:
    a. Supreme Court.
    b. state legislatures.
    c. House of Representatives.
    d. army of the United States.

15. Which of the following is *not* true of the campaign and election of 1800?
    a. It was probably the ugliest in American history.
    b. Parties and party organization played an important role.
    c. It underscored problems in the method of electing a president.
    d. It resulted in a clear victory for the winning candidate.

True/False

Read each statement carefully. Mark true statements "T" and false statements "F."

___1. The most resourceful advocate of a centralized government was Alexander Hamilton.
___2. The intellectual leader of the Constitutional Convention was James Madison.
___3. The "Great Compromise" was important because it solved the problem of representation.
___4. The Constitution did not resolve the question of which law—state or national—would be the supreme law of the land.
___5. Abiding by the rules set up under the Articles of Confederation, the Constitution could not go into effect until it was ratified by all the states in the Union.

___6. The essays known collectively as *The Federalist Papers* called for the ratification of the Constitution.

___7. The Constitution had little chance of success unless it was ratified by Virginia and New York.

___8. After the Constitution was ratified, Americans agreed that the government should strive to create a highly commercial, urban nation.

___9. The Federalist vision for America included government by a wealthy, enlightened ruling class.

___10. Virginia agreed to support Hamilton's "assumption" bill in return for locating the national capital in the South.

___11. Most of the framers of the Constitution believed organized political parties were evil and should be avoided.

___12. The national government's response to the Whiskey Rebellion was to win allegiance through intimidation.

___13. In 1796, Thomas Jefferson ran for vice president on the Federalist ticket.

___14. Aaron Burr's role in the election of 1800 was not very significant.

___15. After the election of 1800, Federalists tried to hold on to power through the federal judiciary.

Review Questions

These questions are to be answered with essays. This will allow you to explore relationships among individuals, events, and attitudes of the period under review.

1. Explain Hamilton's motives for proposing his plans for taxation, assumption, and currency regulation. What was it in his motives that so upset Jefferson and Madison?

2. The Bill of Rights is generally recognized as protecting the citizens of the United States from their government, but what safeguards are contained in the Constitution to protect the states from violations of their rights? What additional safeguards were proposed by Jefferson and Madison in the Virginia and Kentucky Resolutions, and what were the implications of these resolutions with regard to the growth of the central government?

3. Compare and contrast the political, economic, and social philosophies of Thomas Jefferson and Alexander Hamilton. Explain the sort of nation each wished to create.

4. During the period we have just studied, two opposing political parties arose. Both had their roots in the era governed under the

Articles, but unlike competing groups during that period, both factions claimed to support the Constitution. If both felt that the Constitution created the best form of government, what was the basis for their disagreement? Compare and contrast the two parties—their goals, methods, and philosophies. (Be sure to consult earlier chapters when answering this question.)

5. During the Federalist era, events in other countries did much to shape political party growth and domestic policy. Look at American relations with England, Spain, and France; analyze how these relations affected the two political parties that emerged during this period; and explain the way the government responded to this foreign influence on the parties.

CHAPTER SEVEN

The Jeffersonian Era

OBJECTIVES

A thorough study of Chapter 7 should enable you to understand:

1. Thomas Jefferson's views on education, and the role of education in the concept of a "virtuous and enlightened citizenry."
2. The indications of American cultural nationalism that were beginning to emerge during the first two decades of the nineteenth century.
3. The effects of the Revolutionary era on religion, and the changing religious patterns that helped bring on the Second Great Awakening.
4. The evidence noticeable in the first two decades of the 1800s that the nation was not destined to remain the simple, agrarian republic envisioned by the Jeffersonians.
5. The political philosophy of Jefferson, and the extent to which he was able to adhere to his philosophy while president.
6. The Jeffersonian-Federalist struggle over the judiciary—its causes, the main points of conflict, and the importance of the outcome for the future of the nation.
7. President Jefferson's constitutional reservations concerning the Louisiana Purchase, the significance of the decision to accept the bargain, and the importance of the Lewis and Clark expedition.
8. What Thomas Jefferson and James Madison were attempting to accomplish by "peaceable coercion," and why their efforts were not successful.
9. The numerous explanations of the causes of the War of 1812, and why there is so much disagreement among historians.
10. The extent of the opposition to the American war effort, and the ways in which the peace settlement proved satisfactory for most citizens.
11. That America's industrial revolution was part of a global industrial revolution.

PERTINENT QUESTIONS

The Rise of Cultural Nationalism (pp. 168–173)

1. What effect did Republican ideology have on education in the United States?
2. Explain the "cultural independence" that Jeffersonian Americans sought. What means of expression did this "independence" find?
3. What were the obstacles faced by Americans who aspired to create a more elevated national literary life? What efforts were made to overcome these obstacles?
4. How did the American Revolution affect traditional forms of religious practice? What challenges to religious traditionalism arose during this period?
5. What caused the Second Great Awakening?
6. Why were the Methodists, the Baptists, and the Presbyterians so successful on the frontier?
7. What were the "message" and the impact of the Second Great Awakening?

Stirrings of Industrialism (pp. 173–179)

8. What was the industrial revolution? Where and why did it begin?
9. Explain the role that Eli Whitney played in America's industrial revolution. What impact did his inventions have on the South? On the North?
10. What effect did America's transportation system have on industrialization?
11. What were the characteristics of American population growth and expansion in the years between 1790 and 1800?

Jefferson the President (pp. 179–183)

12. How did Jefferson's presidency represent a "fundamental change" in the direction of the federal government?
13. How was the relative "unimportance of the federal government" during the Jefferson administration symbolized by the character of the national capital?
14. What were the characteristics of the "spirit of democratic simplicity" that was the style set by Jefferson for his administration?
15. How did Jefferson combine his duties as president and as party leader in his efforts to govern the country?
16. Why did Jefferson, despite his views on government spending, go to "war" with the pasha of Tripoli? What was the outcome?

17. What were the roots of Jefferson's conflict with the federal court system, and how did the case of *Marbury* v. *Madison* fit into the controversy? What is the significance of *Marbury* v. *Madison*?
18. What method did Jefferson employ to bring the judiciary under Republican control, and what were the results?

Doubling the National Domain (pp. 183–187)

19. Why was New Orleans "the one single spot" that made its possessor the "natural enemy" of the United States?
20. Which group in America was most concerned with the French possession of New Orleans, and how did this concern threaten Jefferson politically?
21. How were the negotiations for the Louisiana Purchase conducted, and what were the terms agreed on?
22. What were the reasons behind Jefferson's reservations over the purchase of Louisiana, and how was he able to reason these doubts away?
23. What was the purpose of the Lewis and Clark expedition, and what did the expedition accomplish?
24. What was the reaction of the New England Federalists to the Louisiana Purchase, and what was their plan to overcome its effects?
25. What were the circumstances that led to the duel between Hamilton and Burr?
26. What was the "Burr conspiracy," and what was its outcome?
27. How do the records kept by Lewis and Clark reflect the purpose of their expedition?

Expansion and War (pp. 188–193)

28. Why was America important to both sides in the conflict between England and France, and what role did the Americans hope to play in the struggle?
29. How did each belligerent nation attempt to prevent America from trading with the other, why was one more successful than the other, and what was the American response?
30. What was Jefferson's response to the *Chesapeake-Leopard* affair, and why did he take this action?
31. How did the Embargo affect the election of 1808, and what was the response of the new president to diplomatic problems that the Embargo had addressed?
32. How did conditions in the West heighten the tension between the United States and Britain?

33. What was Tecumseh's attitude toward the treaties previously negotiated between the United States and various Indian tribes? How did he plan to prevent the expansion of white settlements?
34. Why did Americans blame the British for Indian uprisings on the frontier, and what did frontier settlers see as the best solution to the problem?
35. Why did Americans want to wrest control of Florida from the Spanish? What attempts were made to do this before 1812? Which attempts were successful, and which failed?
36. Who were the "War Hawks," and why were they able to exert such influence on America's drift toward war?

The War of 1812 (pp. 193-197)

37. What were the relative successes and failures of the American military during the first year of the war?
38. How did America's fortunes of war change during 1813 and early 1814, and what were the results of this change?
39. What were the plan and purpose of the British invasion of the United States in 1814? What was the result?
40. Why did New England oppose the War of 1812? Prior to 1814, what did the New England states do to hinder the war effort?
41. What caused the leaders of New England to regard the War of 1812 as a threat to their future as a meaningful force in the United States? What did they propose to remedy this situation?
42. What effect did the Hartford Convention have on the Federalist Party?
43. What was the background to peace negotiations at Ghent? What did both sides initially demand, and why did they finally agree on the terms they did?

IDENTIFICATION

Identify each of the following, and explain why it is important within the context of the chapter.

1. "republican mother"
2. "noble savages"
3. midwifery
4. deism
5. Handsome Lake
6. Robert Fulton
7. Pierre L'Enfant
8. Barbary states

9. John Marshall
10. Lewis and Clark
11. "northern confederacy"
12. General James Wilkinson
13. "peaceable coercion"
14. Macon's Bill No. 2
15. Tecumseh
16. William Henry Harrison
17. Tenskwatawa
18. Battle of Tippecanoe
19. Henry Clay
20. Put-in Bay
21. Battle of Horseshoe Bend
22. Francis Scott Key
23. Battle of New Orleans
24. John Quincy Adams

DOCUMENT

Few inaugural addresses have had the lasting impact of Thomas Jefferson's first inaugural address, which he delivered in early 1801. Some historians have suggested that it was addressed not to his supporters, but to his political enemies. What evidence is there in the excerpt below to suggest that this is true? What evidence is there that this was in keeping with the principles that Jefferson had endorsed as long as he had been in public office? How do the principles espoused here relate to those in the Declaration of Independence? In the Virginia Statute of Religious Liberty?

> We are all Republicans, we are all Federalists. If there be any among us who would wish to dissolve this Union or to change its republican form, let them stand undisturbed as monuments of the safety with which error of opinion may be tolerated where reason is left free to combat it. I know, indeed, that some honest men fear that a republican government can not be strong, that this Government is not strong enough; but would the honest patriot, in the full tide of successful experiment, abandon a government which has so far kept us free and firm on the theoretic and visionary fear that this Government, the world's best hope, may by possibility want energy to preserve itself? I trust not. I believe this, on the contrary, the strongest Government on earth. I believe it the only one where every man, at the call of the law, would fly to the standard of the law, and would meet invasions of the public order as his own personal concern. Sometimes it is said that man can not be trusted with the government of himself. Can he, then, be trusted with the government of others? Or have we found angels in the forms of kings to govern him? Let history answer this question.

MAP EXERCISE

Fill in or identify the following on the blank map provided. Use the map on page 196 of the text as your source.

1. United States and territories belonging to the United States.
2. British America and its principal towns.
3. Spanish Florida and its principal towns.
4. Principal ports on the Atlantic coast.
5. Routes of troop movements.
6. Battle sites and dates, indicating the victor.
7. Extent of the British blockade.

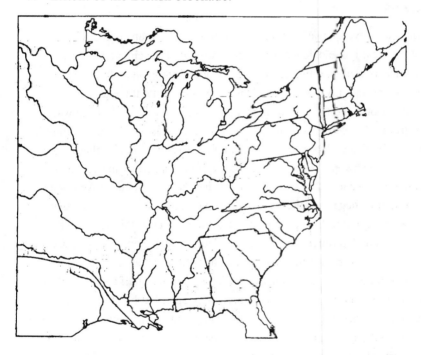

Interpretative Questions

Based on what you have filled in, answer the following. For some of the questions you will need to consult the narrative in your text for information or explanation.

1. Why did northern and southern frontiersmen want to expand into Canada and Florida? How did foreign occupation of these areas hinder western expansion in other regions?

2. Locate the major routes taken by the British when they invaded the United States. What geographic considerations played a part in the choice of where to attack? What made these sites important?
3. Locate the routes taken by American forces. What geographic considerations played a part in the choice of where to attack? What made these sites important?
4. Which region of the country gained the most from the War of 1812? Which felt that it lost as a result of the war? Explain.
5. Study America's expansion into Florida. What impact did the War of 1812 have on this?

SUMMARY

The period just covered was marked by definition and expansion. Having achieved political independence, Americans struggled to achieve cultural independence as well, and this search for self-identity touched almost every phase of the nation's life. "American" tastes in music, literature, and art developed, encouraged by a growing recognition that the United States was different from other countries and that the difference was worth calling attention to. Religious bodies with ties to the old, colonial ways declined as the Second Great Awakening swept America; technology, unrestrained by mercantile rules and regulations, expanded to solve problems that were particularly American; American politics began to take on characteristics and respond to needs that found little precedent in European systems. At the center of this activity, at times leading it and at times being led, was Thomas Jefferson, a president whose versatility seemed to mirror the diversity of the nation. An aristocrat with democratic sentiments, a strict constructionist who bought half a continent, Jefferson was as contradictory as the American people; but like those people, his ultimate goal was the freedom of individuals to pursue their interests, to expand their talents to the fullest. In that sense, Jefferson, although a pragmatic politician, was also a committed idealist—one who deserves to be the symbol of the age that bears his name.

Although Jefferson was out of office when the war between the United States and Britain began, events during his presidency did much to shape the course of the conflict. The War of 1812 did more than test the army and navy of the United States—it tested the nation's ability to survive deep internal divisions and threatened America's independence as surely as did the forces of Great Britain. Hoping to keep the nation out of war, Jefferson and Madison followed a policy that kept the peace but raised fears among their political enemies. Those opponents, their power and influence declining, saw the government's policies as much directed against themselves as the British; as war neared, many came to see it as part of the "plot" as well. In the meantime, the rest of the nation, feeling that Britain was insulting their sovereignty, rallied to President Madison, who brought the conflict to a successful (if somewhat ill-defined) conclusion.

CHAPTER SELF-TEST

After you have read the chapter in the text and done the exercises in the study guide, the following self-test can be taken to see if you understand the material you have covered. Answers appear at the end of the study guide.

Multiple Choice

Circle the letter of the response that best answers the question or completes the statement.

1. In the Republican vision of America, education was essential because:
   a. schools were the best place to teach children to be good party members.
   b. an ignorant electorate could not be trusted to preserve democracy.
   c. business leaders needed to be educated.
   d. schools were where religious values were taught.

2. Early in the eighteenth century religious traditionalists were alarmed over:
   a. a decline in religious education.
   b. the popularity of immoral literature.
   c. demands to separate church and state.
   d. the rise of "rational" religious doctrines.

3. The Second Great Awakening:
   a. combined a more active piety with a belief in a God whose grace could be attained through faith and good works.
   b. turned back the doctrine of predestination.
   c. drew many converts to Unitarianism and Universalism.
   d. had no impact on women and slaves.

4. The work of Eli Whitney:
   a. improved transportation in the South.
   b. led to the expansion of the cotton culture and slavery.
   c. made the South a major textile-producing region.
   d. led to the decline of slavery, for fewer workers were needed to process the cotton.

5. During his administration, Thomas Jefferson:
   a. used the Alien and Sedition Acts against the Federalists.
   b. cut the national debt almost in half.
   c. showed little interest in westward expansion.
   d. made peace with Aaron Burr.

6. With Jefferson in the White House, the last Federalist stronghold was the:
   a. Senate.
   b. House of Representatives.
   c. federal judiciary.
   d. southern states.

7. In the case of *Marbury* v. *Madison,* the Supreme Court:
   a. affirmed its power to nullify an act of Congress.
   b. upheld Adams's right to make "midnight appointments."
   c. confirmed the power of Congress to expand judicial authority.
   d. ordered Madison to deliver Marbury's commission.

8. The greatest accomplishment of Chief Justice John Marshall was that he:
   a. stopped the growth of Republican power.
   b. prevented a Federalist revival in New England.
   c. refused to expand the power of the judiciary.
   d. made the judiciary a coequal branch of government.

9. What possibility concerned Jefferson when he said, "we must marry ourselves to the British fleet and nation"?
   a. An Indian uprising in the Ohio Valley.
   b. The French occupation of New Orleans.
   c. Increased Spanish strength in the Gulf of Mexico.
   d. A war between England, France, and Spain.

10. Jefferson had reservations about buying Louisiana because:
    a. he doubted his constitutional power to do so.
    b. he feared it would upset western Indian tribes.
    c. New Orleans had few Americans living there.
    d. the Spanish claimed the territory as theirs.

11. Americans learned what Louisiana actually was after:
    a. the French gave them detailed maps.
    b. the Lewis and Clark expedition returned.
    c. new states were carved from the territory.
    d. the Spanish allowed it to be explored.

12. Federalists were upset by the Louisiana Purchase because they believed:
    a. it was unconstitutional.
    b. more slave states would come into the Union.
    c. western states would be Republican states.
    d. the British were behind it.

13. The Essex Junto was:
    a. a Federalist organization created to support Jefferson.
    b. the anti-Burr coalition in New York.
    c. a literary club in New England.
    d. a group of radical Federalists who wanted to take New England out of the Union.

14. The Burr-Hamilton duel took place because:
    a. Burr believed Hamilton was responsible for his defeat in the election for the governor of New York.
    b. Hamilton believed Burr was plotting treason.
    c. Burr refused to support Jefferson in 1801.
    d. Hamilton wanted to rid himself of a political rival.

15. The apparent goal of the "Burr conspiracy" was to:
    a. make Burr "king" of the American southwest.
    b. invade Mexico and take it from the Spanish.
    c. return Louisiana to France.
    d. force Jefferson to accept Burr back into the Republican Party.

16. Early in the nineteenth century, the American merchant marine could be described as:
    a. weak and ineffective.
    b. one of the most important in the world.
    c. unable to compete with Britain in the West Indian trade.
    d. of little consequence in the American economy.

17. Jefferson refused to ask for war after the *Chesapeake-Leopard* incident because he:
    a. believed "peaceable coercion" would work.
    b. felt the British were within their rights.
    c. did not want the Federalists to make it an issue.
    d. was against war in general.

18. The Embargo Act hurt which of the following the most?
    a. England
    b. France
    c. New England
    d. The South

19. Jefferson told the Indians of the Northwest they could:
    a. convert themselves to farmers.
    b. move to the West.
    c. continue to live as they always had.
    d. a and b
    e. none of the above

20. The Prophet, Tenskwatawa, was significant because he:
    a. brought Indians to the Christian faith.
    b. inspired an Indian religious revival that helped unite the tribes.
    c. advocated a religious war with southern tribes.
    d. convinced the Indians to accept Jefferson's policies.

21. Tecumseh was important because he:
    a. advocated Indian unity to stop white expansion.
    b. allied the northwestern Indians with the British in Canada.
    c. was able to defeat the Americans at Tippecanoe.
    d. helped his brother, the Prophet, in his religious work.

22. The congressional election of 1810 was important because it:
    a. added a number of young, western, anti-British representatives to the House.
    b. greatly increased the strength of the Republican Party.
    c. brought in a number of peace advocates.
    d. gave rise to a new political party.

23. The United States declaration of war was at first largely ignored by Great Britain because:
    a. England was preoccupied with Napoleon.
    b. the United States could not invade British territory.
    c. England's Indian allies would fight for them
    d. England considered it only a bluff.

24. Apart from the British, the real losers in the War of 1812 were the:
    a. Spanish in Florida and Mexico.
    b. Canadians.
    c. Indian tribes east of the Mississippi River.
    d. Republicans in the West.

25. The Hartford Convention was held in an effort to:
    a. force Republicans to address the grievances New England Federalists had against the Madison administration.
    b. forge an alliance between the Northeast and the West.
    c. convince Republicans in New England that the region should secede from the Union.
    d. reorganize the Federalist Party and pick a candidate for the election of 1816.

True/False

Read each statement carefully. Mark true statements "T" and false statements "F."

___1.   In the Jeffersonian era, schooling was primarily the responsibility of private institutions.

___2.   An argument for the education of women was that they could not be good "republican mothers" unless they were educated themselves.

___3.   Once Americans won political independence from England, they had little interest in cultural independence.

___4.   Early in the nineteenth century most Americans abandoned traditional religious doctrines.

___5.   In the early nineteenth century, industrialization in the United States was hampered by an inadequate transportation system.

___6.   Thomas Jefferson refused to use political office to reward loyal supporters.

___7.   At Jefferson's urging, Justice Samuel Chase was impeached for political reasons, not because he had committed a crime.

___8.   Jefferson wanted to reduce internal taxes, but not abolish them.

___9.   American's strong navy made it unnecessary for the United States to pay tribute to the Barbary states, as weaker nations were doing.

___10. Napoleon's plans for an American empire were blocked by a British invasion of Belgium.

___11. The Louisiana Territory was organized on the same general pattern of the Northwest Territory.

___12. Reports from explorer Zebulon Pike convinced Americans that land between the Missouri River and the Rockies was good for agriculture.

___13. Federalists in New York tried to get Aaron Burr to join them in an anti-Jefferson coalition, but he refused.

___14. The Burr Conspiracy was a plot by a desperate man, acting alone.

___15. Both Jefferson and Marshall wanted Burr convicted for treason.

___16. Americans agreed that the British should be free to search for deserters who might be serving in the American merchant marine.

___17. Americans had little problem with French violations of our neutral rights.

___18. After the *Chesapeake-Leopard* affair, Britain renounced its policy of impressment.

___19. The Harrison Land Law of 1800 made it possible for white settlers to acquire farms from the public domain on easier terms than before.

___20. Under Jefferson's Indian policy the tribes were granted their tribal lands forever.

___21. The Indians in the West would not have risen against the United States if the British in Canada had not told them to do so.

___22. White southerners wanted Florida because it blocked river access to the Gulf of Mexico.

___23. American troops invaded Canada and held it for the entire War of 1812.

___24. As a result of the Battle of New Orleans the United States was able to force Britain to sign the Treaty of Ghent.

___25. In the Treaty of Ghent, England formally renounced impressment.

Review Questions

These questions are to be answered with essays. This will allow you to explore relationships among individuals, events, and attitudes of the period under review.

1. Considering the variety of movements covered in the section of your text entitled "The Rise in Cultural Nationalism," how did American cultural life in the early nineteenth century reflect the Republican vision of the nation's future?

2. Jefferson and the Republicans championed the rights of the states and advocated a strict adherence to the Constitution, but once in office, they found new situations that demanded governmental actions that, in some cases, went beyond what the Federalists had done. What caused Jefferson and his party to change their approach to governing, what reservations did they have about what they were doing, and how were they able to rationalize this apparent change in program and philosophy? (Be sure to consult previous chapters when answering this question.)

3. How did the Federalists respond to Republican programs? If the Federalists favored a loose interpretation of the Constitution, why did they protest when Jefferson used a loose interpretation as well? What was it in the Republican program that the Federalists saw as a threat, and how did they respond?

4. Many historians view the War of 1812 as the "second American war for independence," but is this an accurate characterization? In what

way did British policies prior to 1812 threaten our independence? Had the United States not fought the war, what might the results have been? Assess these questions, and determine if the United States was indeed fighting for "independence."

5. What happened to the Federalists? For the first decade under the Constitution, the Federalist Party held the nation together, started the government working on a day-to-day basis, and set precedents that are still valid. Twenty years later, they had all but ceased to exist as a party. Why? Examine the events and issues that accompanied the decline of the Federalists, and determine what caused this powerful party to fall. (Be sure to consult the previous chapter when answering this question.)

CHAPTER EIGHT
Varieties of American Nationalism

OBJECTIVES

A thorough study of Chapter 8 should enable you to understand:

1. The effects of the War of 1812 on banking, shipping, farming, industry, and transportation.
2. Postwar governmental efforts to improve banking and transportation.
3. The westward expansion after the War of 1812 and its relation to the growing interest in internal improvements.
4. The settlement patterns that resulted from this postwar westward expansion.
5. The "era of good feelings" as a transitional period.
6. The causes of the Panic of 1819, and the effects of the subsequent depression on politics and the economy.
7. The arguments advanced by North and South during the debates over the admission of Missouri, and how they were to influence sectional attitudes.
8. The ways in which the status of the federal judiciary was changed by the Marshall Court, and how the Court's decision altered the relationships between the federal government and the states and the federal government and business.
9. The reasons why President James Monroe announced his "doctrine" in 1823, and its impact on international relations at the time.
10. Presidential politics in the "era of good feelings," and how they altered the political system.
11. The frustrations experienced by John Quincy Adams during his term as president.
12. The reasons why Andrew Jackson was elected in 1828, and the significance of his victory.

PERTINENT QUESTIONS

Stabilizing Economic Growth (pp. 201–204)

1. How did America's wartime experience underline the need for another national bank?
2. How did Congress propose to promote manufacturing in the United States?
3. How was transportation improved during this period? What serious gaps remained in the nation's transportation system?
4. What were the arguments in favor of internal improvements financed by the government? What were the arguments against this idea?

Expanding Westward (pp. 204–208)

5. What were the reasons for the so-called great migration?
6. What were the characteristics of life among white settlers in the Old Northwest?
7. How did life in the Old Southwest differ from that in other sections of the country?
8. Who were the "mountain men"? Why were they important in the settlement of the West?
9. Explain the perception that easterners had of the West.

The "Era of Good Feelings" (pp. 208–211)

10. Why were the leaders of New England disturbed at the nomination and election of James Monroe for president, and what did Monroe do to calm these fears?
11. Why was Florida such a problem for Americans in the South, and how did Andrew Jackson make the resolution of the problem an absolute necessity?
12. What were the critical points decided by the Adams-Onís negotiations?
13. What were the causes of the Panic of 1819?
14. What impact did the Panic of 1819 have on the American economy? What did the government do to try to ease the pain of this depression?

Sectionalism and Nationalism (pp. 211–217)

15. What were the major elements of disagreement in the debate over the admission of Missouri into the Union?
16. Which group opposed Missouri's entering the Union as a slave state? Why?

17. What was the Missouri Compromise? Why did nationalists regard it as a "happy resolution of a danger to the Union"? Why were others less optimistic?

18. What was the net effect of the opinions delivered by the Marshall Court? How did these opinions reflect John Marshall's philosophy of government?

19. Who led the opposition to the Marshall Court, and what was the position they took in denouncing it?

20. What was the long-range significance of the case of *Gibbons* v. *Ogden*? Of immediate importance, how did this case help to blunt criticism of the Court?

21. How was it that the United States's proclamation of neutrality in the wars between Spain and its colonies actually aided the colonies? Why did the United States do this?

22. Read the section in the text on the Monroe Doctrine, and answer these three questions:
    a. Why did the president announce the "doctrine" when he did?
    b. What specific dangers, if any, did he have in mind when he announced the "doctrine"?
    c. Against what powers in particular was his warning directed?

The Revival of Opposition (pp. 217–219)

23. Why was the caucus system viewed with such disdain before the election of 1824?

24. Who were the candidates in the election of 1824? What was the platform of each?

25. What was the outcome of the election of 1824? How was that result arrived at, and what part did Henry Clay play in it?

26. What was the "corrupt bargain," and why did it take place?

27. What did John Quincy Adams plan to accomplish during his presidency? What role was the federal government to play in these plans? Was he successful? Why or why not?

28. In the field of foreign affairs, what did Adams and Clay attempt to do? Were they successful? Why or why not?

29. What problems brought on the tariff debates of 1827 and 1828? In what way did the South respond to northeastern demands for a higher tariff, and on what did the antitariff forces base their stand?

30. What was the outcome of these tariff debates, and why was it that few were pleased with these results?

31. How had Andrew Jackson's supporters prepared for the election of 1828? What were the issues in the campaign, and what was the outcome?

32. Who were the National Republicans? Who were their leaders? What programs did they support, and from what areas did they draw their strength?

IDENTIFICATION

Identify each of the following, and explain why it is important within the context of the chapter.

1. Second Bank of the United States
2. Francis C. Lowell
3. National Road
4. Rocky Mountain Fur Company
5. Monroe's good will tour
6. Tallmadge Amendment
7. *Fletcher* v. *Peck*
8. *Dartmouth College* v. *Woodward*
9. *McCullough* v. *Maryland*
10. *Worcester* v. *Georgia*
11. "King Caucus"
12. "coffin handbill"

MAP EXERCISE

Fill in or identify the following on the blank map provided. Use the map on page 212 of the text as your source.

1. Free states and territories in 1820.
2. Slave states and territories in 1820.
3. Missouri Compromise line.
4. Dates states entered the Union.
5. Territory closed to slavery by the Missouri Compromise.
6. Territory open to slavery by the Missouri Compromise.
7. Mexico, British America, and Oregon.

Interpretative Questions

Based on what you have filled in, answer the following. For some of the
questions you will need to consult the narrative in your text for information or
explanation.

1. What migration and settlement patterns helped determine that
   Missouri would want to enter the Union as a slave state?
2. What impact did the manner in which states were previously
   admitted to the Union have on the reaction to the admission of
   Missouri?
3. Why would the South accept the Missouri Compromise? What does
   this tell you about the nature of the plantation system and attitudes
   toward the institution of slavery and its ability to expand?
4. What potential existed (as a result of the Missouri Compromise) for
   an eventual upsetting of the balance between slave and free states?
   Which section seemed to gain the most from this?
5. How did the Missouri Compromise reflect the tensions between
   political parties at the time, especially tensions that were the result of
   the expansion of the nation?

SUMMARY

After the War of 1812 a new spirit of nationalism and expansion emerged, and the nation, led by a president determined to heal old wounds, embarked on an "era of good feelings." Unfortunately, there were many who did not feel very good for very long. During the 1820s two forces, one divisive and the other unifying, shaped American life and politics. The first appeared during the Missouri debates, which, despite overtones that resembled the earlier Federalist-Republican clashes, brought the issue of slavery and its expansion to the forefront. The immediate question—which section (North or South) would control the Senate—was dealt with through the Missouri Compromise, but the underlying problem was more difficult to resolve. What the debates revealed was that some in the nation saw the addition of slave states (not just western states, but slave states) as a threat. Southern politicians, it was apparent, had come to equate the expansion of slavery with the expansion of their own political philosophy (and power). How true these beliefs were is not the issue. What is important is that they were believed, and, as the years passed, more would come to share these convictions. Countering this divisive force was the spirit of nationalism and the emergence of two parties—both with a national following. These developments seemed to overshadow sectional concerns, and with the election of Andrew Jackson, one of the most popular political figures since George Washington, the nation seemed more concerned with unity than division. How long this was to last was another question.

CHAPTER SELF-TEST

After you have read the chapter in the text and done the exercises in the study guide, the following self-test can be taken to see if you understand the material you have covered. Answers appear at the end of the study guide.

Multiple Choice

Circle the letter of the response that best answers the question or completes the statement.

1. Which of the following did *not* occur after the War of 1812?
   a. Commerce revived and expanded.
   b. An economic boom was followed by a disastrous bust.
   c. All banking was left to the states.
   d. Westward expansion accelerated dramatically

2. After peace was restored, American industries that prospered during the war:
    a. were strong enough to withstand British competition.
    b. expanded into foreign markets.
    c. were competitive with foreign imports.
    d. demanded that the government protect them from foreign competition.

3. After the war, the nation's most pressing economic need was:
    a. access to foreign markets that were not open to American commerce.
    b. a trained labor force to work in complex industries.
    c. a transportation system that would provide manufacturers access to raw materials and markets.
    d. a system by which worn out soil could be reclaimed.

4. Which of the following was *not* a reason behind the "great migration" after the War of 1812?
    a. Population increase
    b. Free land
    c. Weakening Indian resistance
    d. Economic pressure

5. Farmers seemed to prefer land in the Old Northwest rather than the Southwest because:
    a. the spread of the plantation system limited opportunity in the South.
    b. Indians were still active in the South.
    c. the Northwest had richer soil.
    d. land was cheaper in the Northwest.

6. As far as most Americans were concerned, the area west of the Mississippi was:
    a. a "Great American Desert."
    b. the next great agricultural frontier.
    c. too far from towns and cities to be attractive.
    d. fit only for a plantation-style economy.

7. The administration of President James Monroe was called the Era of Good Feelings because:
    a. it was a time of few factional disputes and partisan divisions.
    b. there were no economic depressions.
    c. most Americans were content to remain where they were.
    d. the national bank successfully managed the economy.

8. Because he favored American expansion, John Quincy Adams:
   a. called on the United States to occupy Oregon.
   b. felt a war with Mexico would help the nation's economy.
   c. supported Jackson's invasion of Florida.
   d. was unwilling to give up claims to Texas.

9. Although the Panic of 1819 had many causes, the West assigned the primary blame for the panic on:
   a. state banks.
   b. land speculators.
   c. the national bank.
   d. Congress.

10. John Marshall's influence on the Supreme Court was so great that he:
    a. was able to get whomever he wanted appointed to the bench.
    b. more than anyone other than the framers themselves molded the development of the Constitution.
    c. was able to ignore the other justices.
    d. could single-handedly overturn acts of Congress.

11. The lasting significance of *Gibbons* v. *Ogden* was that it:
    a. opened the way for steamboat travel on the Mississippi.
    b. confirmed the states' right to regulate commerce.
    c. made peace between the court and the Adams administration.
    d. freed transportation systems from restraints by the states.

12. The decisions of the Marshall Court:
    a. established the primacy of the federal government in regulating the economy.
    b. gave strength to the doctrine of states' rights.
    c. destroyed what was left of Hamiltonian Federalism.
    d. opened the way for an increased federal role in promoting economic growth.
    e. a and d
    f. b and c

13. In its rulings concerning the Indian tribes, the Marshall Court held that:
    a. the national government, not the states, had authority.
    b. Indians were citizens like everyone else.
    c. Indians had the same status as slaves.
    d. tribal lands belong to the states.

14. The charge of a "corrupt bargain" was raised when:
    a. Clay supported Adams for the presidency and was appointed secretary of state.
    b. Jackson promised to reward his supporters if he won.
    c. Adams won with the support of southern planters.
    d. the Republican caucus threw its support to Adams.

15. Adams's "nationalistic program," which was a lot like Clay's "American System," was not funded because:
    a. the nation could not afford it.
    b. business opposed it.
    c. western interests opposed it.
    d. Jackson's supporters in Congress voted against it.

True/False

Read each statement carefully. Mark true statements "T" and false statements "F."

___1. Difficulties in financing the War of 1812 underlined the need for a national bank.

___2. Tariffs were generally favored by manufacturing interests but opposed by those who made their living from agriculture.

___3. One reason for the growing interest in internal improvements was the sudden and dramatic surge in westward expansion in the years following the War of 1812.

___4. The advance of the southern frontier meant the spread not just of cotton but also of slavery.

___5. During this period there was very little economic opportunity for Americans who wanted to trade with the far Southwest and Mexico.

___6. Andrew Jackson took Florida and the Adams-Onís Treaty made it legal.

___7. The Missouri Compromise upset the balance between slave and free states.

___8. In *McCulloch* v. *Maryland* the Supreme Court declared the national bank unconstitutional.

___9. The decision in *Gibbon* v. *Ogden* was popular because it was a stand against monopoly power.

___10. The Marshall Court's rulings concerning the Indian tribes were among its most popular decisions.

___11. The Monroe Doctrine was passed by Congress and immediately became an important part of our foreign policy.

___12. The political divisions that appeared in the late 1820s were in no way related to the divisions of the 1790s.

___13. Henry Clay's "American System" included a national bank, a protective tariff, and federally funded internal improvements.

___14. In 1828, Andrew Jackson lost the presidential election because he was too closely identified with an "economic aristocracy" that his enemies claimed controlled him.

Review Questions

These questions are to be answered with essays. This will allow you to explore relationships among individuals, events, and attitudes of the period under review.

1. After the War of 1812, there emerged a group of Republicans who urged the nation to consider "national" issues rather than "local" or "sectional" matters. So persistent were they that many of their party contended that they were abandoning the basic principles laid down by Jefferson. Were they? Could this new group be called "Jeffersonian," or did it represent something else? Examine the things the nationalists proposed for the nation, then go back to Chapter 6 and compare their plans with those of Jefferson and Hamilton. To which set of plans does the nationalists' program seem more closely allied? What does this tell you about the nature of political parties and political ideas at this time? Also, how does the emergence of the nationalists relate to the decline of the Federalists?

2. Nationalism was a unifying factor in the 1820s, but how did this nationalistic attitude, which was so evident in domestic affairs, influence foreign policy? What were the effects of nationalism on American foreign policy during this period, and what forces, if any, tended to negate its influence?

3. How did the career of John Marshall contribute to the rise of nationalism during this era? In what specific areas did he increase the power of the national government? Of the two political parties, which was more likely to support Marshall? Why?

CHAPTER NINE

Jacksonian America

OBJECTIVES

A thorough study of Chapter 9 should enable you to understand:

1. Andrew Jackson's philosophy of government, and his impact on the office of the presidency.
2. The nullification theory of John C. Calhoun, and President Jackson's reaction to the attempt to put nullification into action.
3. The supplanting of John C. Calhoun by Martin Van Buren as successor to Jackson, and the significance of the change.
4. The reasons for the Jacksonian war on the Bank of the United States, and the effects of Jackson's veto on the powers of the president and on the American financial system.
5. The causes of the Panic of 1837, and the effect of the panic on the presidency of Van Buren.
6. The differences in party philosophy between the Democrats and the Whigs, the reasons for the Whig victory in 1840, and the effect of the election on political campaigning.
7. The negotiations that led to the Webster-Ashburton Treaty, and the importance of the treaty in Anglo-American relations.
8. The reasons why John C. Calhoun, Henry Clay, and Daniel Webster were never able to reach their goal—the White House.

PERTINENT QUESTIONS

The Rise of Mass Politics (pp. 223–227)

1. What were the general characteristics of "Jacksonian Democracy," its philosophy, and its practice?
2. What role did the western states play in the growing democratization of American politics?
3. What was the reaction of the older states to these democratic trends? Cite some examples.
4. What groups were excluded from this widening of political opportunity? Why?

5. How did the spoils system fit into Jackson's "democratic" plans? What other means did he use to bring more people into the political process?
6. What was the effect of this growth of democracy? How did it change, or not change, the American political system? What is its significance?
7. How has the debate over Jacksonian Democracy focused not only on Andrew Jackson but on American society in the Jacksonian era as well?

"Our Federal Union" (pp. 227–231)

8. What was the dilemma faced by John C. Calhoun, and what factors gave rise to it?
9. How did Calhoun attempt to resolve this dilemma? What arguments did he use, and on which sources did he draw?
10. What did Calhoun really hope his theory of nullification would accomplish?
11. How did Martin Van Buren's and John C. Calhoun's backgrounds and rise to prominence differ?
12. What was the Kitchen Cabinet? Who were its members? Why did it come into existence?
13. What were the origins of the Calhoun-Jackson split? How did the Eaton administration contribute to the division? What effect did it have on the Jackson administration?
14. How did the Webster-Hayne debate fit into the controversy between Jackson and Calhoun? What brought about the debate, what was the major point of disagreement between the two, and what were the arguments advanced?
15. How did Calhoun and South Carolina propose to test the theory of nullification? What factors contributed to their decision?
16. What was Jackson's reaction to South Carolina's attempt at nullification? How did his action in this case correspond to his action in the case of the Cherokee removal? What accounts for this?
17. What was the outcome of the nullification crisis? What, if anything, did the antagonists learn from the confrontation?
18. Explain Jackson's position on states' rights. How did he apply this to the matter of internal improvements?

The Removal of the Indians (pp. 231–235)

19. What was the program (inherited by Jackson) designed to deal with the Indians who lived east of the Mississippi? What happened when this program was applied to the Cherokee in Georgia?

20. How did Jackson's action in the matter of the Cherokee removal correspond to his views on the role of the president and on the issue of states' rights?
21. Explain the different ways the Indians responded to Jackson's policies. What was the outcome for the different tribes?
22. How did white Americans justify their policies toward Native Americans. What evidence is there to suggest that there were other alternatives available to expanding Americans?

Jackson and the Bank War (pp. 235–237)

23. What was Jackson's opinion on the Bank of the United States? On what did he base his views? What other factors contributed to his stand?
24. What was Nicholas Biddle's initial attitude toward the Bank's involvement in politics? What caused him to change his mind, what steps did he take, and who were his supporters?
25. How did Jackson respond to the efforts to recharter the Bank? What reasons did he give for his action, and what effect did the election of 1832 have on his Bank policy?
26. How did the supporters of the Bank respond to Jackson's action? What did Biddle do? What were the results?
27. How did the Supreme Court under Roger B. Taney differ from the Court under Marshall? What groups profited from Taney's decisions?

The Emergence of the Second Party System (pp. 238–240)

28. How did the party philosophy of the Whigs differ from that of the Democrats?
29. Who were the Whig leaders? How do they reflect the variety of political opinions found in the Whig Party?
30. What was the Whig strategy in the election of 1836? Who was the Democratic candidate? Why was he selected? What was the result?

Politics After Jackson (pp. 240–245)

31. What was the general condition of the American economy in 1836? What factors contributed to this? What was the most pressing problem that Congress and the administration faced between 1835 and 1837, and how did they propose to solve it?
32. What caused the Panic of 1837? What effect did it have on the nation? On the Democratic Party?
33. What programs did Martin Van Buren propose to ease the depression? Why did he act in this way?

34. Why did the Whigs select William Henry Harrison as their candidate in 1840? How did his campaign "set a new pattern for presidential contests"?
35. What did the selection of John Tyler as Harrison's vice-presidential candidate reveal about the composition of the Whig Party?
36. What was the origin of the split between Tyler and Clay? What effect did it have on the administration? On the Whig Party? What was the result?
37. Why did Daniel Webster not resign from the Tyler cabinet when the other Whigs did? What were the diplomatic problems on which he was working?
38. What were the accomplishments of Webster as secretary of state?

IDENTIFICATION

Identify each of the following, and explain why it is important within the context of the chapter.

1. "The reign of King 'Mob'"
2. Dorr Rebellion
3. Albany Regency
4. William L. Marcy
5. Peggy Eaton
6. Webster's "Second Reply to Hayne"
7. Democrats' Jefferson banquet
8. force bill
9. Black Hawk War
10. Five Civilized Tribes
11. Trail of Tears
12. "soft money"/"hard money"
13. bank war
14. Anti-Mason Party
15. specie circular
16. independent treasury
17. "log cabin" campaign
18. *Caroline* affair
19. Aroostook War
20. Creole
21. Webster-Ashburton Treaty

DOCUMENT

Below is an excerpt from Daniel Webster's reply to Robert Y. Hayne's defense of the theory of nullification. What does Webster see as the danger inherent in Calhoun's doctrine? How is this speech in keeping with Webster's political views, especially his view of the nature of the Union and the role of the national government?

> I have not allowed myself, Sir, to look beyond the Union, to see what might lie hidden in the dark recess behind. I have not coolly weighed the chances of preserving liberty when the bonds that unite us together shall be broken asunder. I have not accustomed myself to hang over the precipice of disunion, to see whether, with my short sight, I can fathom the depth of the abyss below; nor could I regard her as a safe counsellor in the affairs of this government, whose thoughts should be mainly bent on considering, not how the Union may be best preserved, but how tolerable might be the condition of the people when it should be broken up and destroyed. While the Union lasts, we have high, exciting, gratifying prospects spread out before us, for us and our children. Beyond that I seek not to penetrate the veil. God grant that in my day, at least, that curtain may not rise! God grant that on my vision never may be opened what lies behind! When my eyes shall be turned to behold for the last time the sun in heaven, may I not see him shining on the broken and dishonored fragments of a once gorgeous Union; on States dissevered, discordant, and belligerent; on a land rent with civil feuds, or drenched, it may be, in fraternal blood! Let their last feeble and lingering glance rather behold the glorious ensign of the republic, now known and honored throughout the earth, still full high advanced, its arms and trophies steaming in their original lustre, not a stripe erased or polluted, not a single star obscured, bearing for its motto, no such miserable interrogatory as "What is all this worth?" nor those other words of delusion and folly, "Liberty first and Union afterwards"; but everywhere, spread all over in characters of living Light, blazing on its ample folds, as they float over the sea and over the land, and in every wind under the whole heavens, that other sentiment, dear to every true American heart,—Liberty *and* Union, now and for ever, one and inseparable!

Daniel Webster, *The Writings and Speeches of Daniel Webster*, National Edition (Boston, 1903), 6:75.

MAP EXERCISE

Fill in or identify the following on the blank map provided. Use the map on page 234 of the text as your source.

1. Tribal lands and the states and territories in which they were located.
2. Other states in the region.
3. Removal routes (including the towns and forts along the way).
4. Reservations and the forts within them.

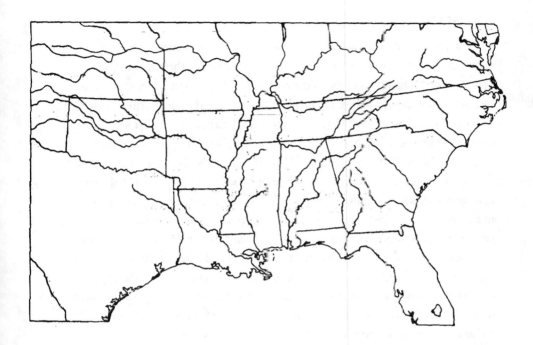

Interpretative Questions

Based on what you have filled in, answer the following. For some of the
questions you will need to consult the narrative in your text for information or
explanation.

1. Why did the states involved want the Indians removed? Look at the
   location of the tribal lands and explain why their continued
   occupation by the Indians represented not only the loss to the state of
   valuable territory but might also threaten the westward movement
   itself.
2. How did the land to which the Indians were removed differ from that
   on which they had lived? Were whites aware of the significance of
   the difference? What does this suggest about white attitudes toward
   the Indians?
3. Note the removal routes. What geographic features were considered
   in determining where the Indians would travel? Do you feel this
   made the trek easier or more difficult?
4. What geographic features made it possible for the Seminoles (and
   some Cherokees) to resist removal?
5. Note the location of the forts in or near the Indian Territory. Why
   were they placed as they were? What does this indicate about
   American Indian policy?

SUMMARY

At first glance, Andrew Jackson seems a study in contradictions: an advocate of states' rights who forced South Carolina to back down in the nullification controversy; a champion of the West who vetoed legislation that would have opened easy access to part of the area and who issued the specie circular, which brought the region's "flush times" to a disastrous halt; a nationalist who allowed Georgia to ignore the Supreme Court; and a defender of majority rule who vetoed the Bank after the majority's representatives, the Congress, had passed it. Perhaps he was, as his enemies argued, simply out for himself. But in the end, few would argue that Andrew Jackson was not a popular president, if not so much for what he did as for what he was. Jackson symbolized what Americans perceived (or wished) themselves to be—defiant, bold, independent. He was someone with whom they could identify. So what if the image was a bit contrived, it was still a meaningful image. Thus Jackson was reelected by an overwhelming majority and was able to transfer that loyalty to his successor, a man who hardly lived up to the image. But all this left a curious question unanswered. Was this new democracy voting for leaders whose programs they favored or, rather, for images that could be altered and manipulated almost at will? The answer was essential for the future of American politics, and the election of 1840 gave the nation a clue.

CHAPTER SELF-TEST

After you have read the chapter in the text and done the exercises in the study guide, the following self-test can be taken to see if you understand the material you have covered. Answers appear at the end of the study guide.

Multiple Choice

Circle the letter of the response that best answers the question or completes the statement.

1. The goal of the Jacksonians was to:
   a. redistribute the wealth of the nation.
   b. reduce the influence of southern planters.
   c. ensure that people could rise to prominence on the basis of their own talents and energies.
   d. put as many of their own people in office as possible.

2. During the Jacksonian era, the number of voters:
   a. increased at a more rapid pace than did the population as a whole.
   b. increased at a slower pace than in the previous decade.

c. actually decreased as a percentage of the population.
d. remained stable.

3. The most significant change regarding "party" to take place in the Jacksonian era was the:
   a. recognition of the value of "third parties."
   b. view that institutionalized parties were a desirable part of the political process.
   c. view that party leaders should be presidential candidates.
   d. emergence of a hard core of party loyalists who picked all candidates for national office.

4. Which of the following did Jackson and the Jacksonians *not* attack?
   a. A "class" of permanent officeholders
   b. The system by which presidential candidates were selected
   c. The "spoils system"
   d. The party caucus

5. John C. Calhoun advanced the theory of nullification as:
   a. a moderate alternative to secession.
   b. a means of making the national government secondary to the states.
   c. a concession to western interests.
   d. a way to force Congress to pass a protective tariff

6. The most significant result of the Eaton affair was that:
   a. John C. Calhoun became the leader of the Kitchen Cabinet.
   b. it led to the Webster-Hayne debate.
   c. Martin Van Buren emerged as Jackson's choice to succeed him.
   d. John Eaton became Jackson's secretary of state.

7. Robert Y. Hayne supported the continued sale of western lands in an effort to:
   a. aid the expansion of slavery.
   b. help finance internal improvements.
   c. add to the deposits in the national bank
   d. get western support for efforts to reduce the tariff.

8. Daniel Webster's "Second Reply to Hayne" was made in an attempt to:
   a. refute Calhoun's theory of nullification.
   b. affirm the integrity of the Union.
   c. support the sale of western lands.
   d. a and b
   e. b and c

9. The "force bill" of 1832:
   a. authorized the president to use force to see that acts of Congress were obeyed.
   b. forced Jackson to stand up to Calhoun.
   c. forced the president to consult Congress if he planned to use troops against South Carolina.
   d. made it impossible for other southern states to nullify laws.

10. When the Indian removal was completed:
   a. every Indian west of the Mississippi River was gone.
   b. only elements of the Seminoles and Cherokees remained.
   c. the Indians were relocated to reservations much like the tribal lands they left.
   d. the Indians were far enough removed from whites where they would not face further encroachments.

11. Under Nicholas Biddle, the national bank:
   a. withheld credit from new businesses.
   b. had a restraining effect on less well-managed state banks.
   c. did little general banking business.
   d. operated solely from its Philadelphia headquarters.

12. The national bank was supported by:
   a. "hard money" advocates.
   b. "soft money" advocates.
   c. western farmers.
   d. eastern business interests.

13. Determined to reduce the Bank's power even before its charter expired, Jackson:
   a. fired most of its officials, including Biddle.
   b. removed government deposits from the Bank.
   c. removed government deposits from state banks.
   d. exposed the high officials who had been borrowing from the Bank.

14. Roger B. Taney's tenure as chief justice:
   a. marked a sharp break with the Marshall Court in constitutional interpretation.
   b. was little more than an extension of the Marshall Court.
   c. helped modify Marshall's vigorous nationalism.
   d. was greatly influenced by the views of John C. Calhoun.

15. The Whig Party:
   a. favored expanding the power of the federal government.
   b. encouraged industrial and commercial development.

c. advocated knitting the country together into a consolidated economic system.

d. All of the above

e. None of the above

True/False

Read each statement carefully. Mark true statements "T" and false statements "F."

___1. If the Jacksonians were consistent in nothing else, they were consistent Democrats.

___2. During the age of Jackson politics became open to virtually all the nation's white male citizens.

___3. Jackson wanted to weaken the functions of the federal government and give the states more power.

___4. Calhoun wanted his nullification theory to be put to the test as soon as possible.

___5. Andrew Jackson's "Kitchen Cabinet" was a group of men the president wanted to have as little to do with as possible.

___6. When South Carolina nullfied the tariffs of 1828 and 1832, Jackson had no choice but to go along.

___7. If Calhoun and his allies learned nothing else from the nullification crisis, they learned that no state could defy the federal government alone.

___8. During the first decades of the nineteenth century the American view of Indians as "noble savages" changed to a view of them simply as "savages."

___9. Indian removal was a purely Jacksonian idea.

___10. Jackson believed the national bank was a citadel of privilege and he was determined to destroy it.

___11. Clay was able to use Jackson's veto of the Bank to defeat him for the presidency.

___12. When the Bank of the United States died in 1836, the country was left with a fragmented and chronically unstable banking system.

___13. The Democratic Party looked with suspicion on government efforts to stimulate commercial and industrial growth.

___14. The Whig vision of America was one of a nation embracing the industrial future and rising to world greatness as a commercial and manufacturing power.

___15. The Van Buren presidency was successful because he was able to quickly bring the nation out of the Panic of 1837.

___16. The 1840 campaign illustrated how getting elected had become as important as governing.

___17. Though Harrison died soon after he took office, John Tyler pushed ahead with Whig programs.

Review Questions

These questions are to be answered with essays. This will allow you to explore relationships among individuals, events, and attitudes of the period under review.

1. Andrew Jackson thought of himself as the "president of the people." Was he? What can you find in the career of Jackson that would support his assertion, and what can you find to deny it?

2. How did white Americans' attitudes toward Native Americans evolve during the early nineteenth century? What factors led to the decision to remove the Indians from land east of the Mississippi? What other alternatives were available, and why were they rejected? How did the Indians respond to the government's policy toward them? (Be sure to consult previous chapters when answering this question.)

3. What was the ostensible reason for the split between Calhoun and Jackson? The Eaton affair is generally seen as a symptom, not a cause, which would indicate that the real division between the two men was much deeper. Assess the causes of the split, and speculate on its significance for the South and for the Democrats.

4. How did William Henry Harrison win in 1840? What were the issues that worked against him, and how did his party exploit them? Furthermore, how was this candidate presented to the people? What image were his managers trying to create, and what does this image tell you about the American electorate?

5. How did Calhoun (and South Carolina) justify and explain the theory of nullification? On what historical precedents could this theory be based? On what points did Webster (and Jackson) oppose this theory? (Be sure to consult previous chapters when answering this question. Pay particular attention to the debate over the Alien and Sedition Acts.)

CHAPTER TEN

America's Economic Revolution

OBJECTIVES

A thorough study of Chapter 10 should enable you to understand:

1. The changes that were taking place within the nation in terms of population growth, population movement, urbanization, and the impact of immigration.
2. The importance of the Erie Canal for the development of the West and of New York City.
3. The changes that were taking place in transportation, business, industry, labor, and commerce as the full impact of the industrial revolution was felt in the United States.
4. The reasons why the Northeast and Northwest tended to become more dependent on each other, while the South became isolated from the rest of the nation in the 1840s and 1850s.
5. The forces behind the rise of the factory and why this was the most profound economic development to take place in mid-nineteenth-century America.
6. The vast changes taking place in the Northeast as agriculture declined while urbanization and industrialization progressed at a rapid rate.
7. The characteristics of the greatly increased immigration of the 1840s and 1850s, and the immigrants' effects on the development of the free states.
8. The reasons for the appearance of the nativist movement in the 1850s.
9. The living and working conditions of both men and women in the northern factory towns and on the northwestern farms.

PERTINENT QUESTIONS

The Changing American Population (pp. 249–253)

1. What were the reasons for and the effect of the rapid increase in population between 1820 and 1840?
2. Where did this increased population settle? What population shifts took place between 1820 and 1840, and how did they affect political division?
3. Why was the rise of New York City so phenomenal? What forces combined to make it America's leading city?
4. What major immigrant groups came to the United States during this period? What impact did they have on the character and distribution of the population in the North?
5. What impact did this immigration have on the political system? Which party was the most successful in attracting immigrant voters? Why?
6. What gave rise to the nativist movement? What were its political goals?

Transportation and Communications Revolutions (pp. 253–259)

7. Why were natural means of carrying commerce (lakes and rivers) unsatisfactory to most Americans?
8. How did Americans propose to overcome the geographical limitations on water travel?
9. Which area took the lead in canal development? What was the effect of these canals on that section of the country? How did other sections respond to this example?
10. What were the general characteristics of early railroad development in the United States? What innovations aided the progress of railroads, and what advantages did railroads have over other forms of transportation?
11. What innovations in transportation and/or communication, other than the growth of the railroads, took place during this period?

Commerce and Industry (pp. 259–262)

12. In the broadening of business described here, what shifts in manufacturing took place and what business innovations occurred, and what effect did this have on the general distribution of goods in America?
13. What influence did technology have on the growth of American industry?

14. What changes contributed to the rise of the factory? Why was this "the most profound economic development in mid-nineteenth-century America"?
15. How did technology and industrial ingenuity prepare the way for the expansion of industry and the growth of the American economy?
16. Who were the "merchant capitalists" and what was the significance of their transformation into "industrial capitalists"?

Men and Women at Work (pp. 262–266)

17. How did the textile mills recruit and use labor? What was the general response of workers to the Lowell method? Of observers? What caused the breakdown of this system?
18. What was the lot of working women in Lowell and other factory towns? How did this differ from conditions in Europe? What problems did these women have in adjusting to factory and factory-town life?
19. How did the circumstances of immigrant workers differ from those of native laborers?
20. What was the general condition of workers in northeastern factories? What impact did factory work have on the artisan tradition in America?
21. What attempts were made to better conditions in northeastern factories? What role did unions play in these attempts, and what was accomplished?

Patterns of Society (pp. 266–273)

22. Why was the increasing wealth of America not widely or equitably distributed? How was this unequal distribution manifested in daily life? Which groups were most likely to be found at the bottom of the economic scale?
23. What was life like for middle-class Americans during the antebellum era?
24. Despite the gap between rich and poor, there was little overt class conflict in antebellum America. Why?
25. What "profound change in the nature and function of the family" took place during this era? What caused this change?
26. What conditions put women in a "separate sphere," and what were the characteristics of the "distinctive female culture" women developed?
27. What was the "cult of domesticity," and what costs and benefits did it bring to middle-class women? To working-class women?

The Agricultural North (pp. 273–277)

28. What caused the decline of farming in the Northeast? What did farmers in the Northeast do to overcome this decline, and what new patterns in agriculture resulted?
29. What was the basis of the economy in the Northwest? What goods were produced there?
30. Where were most of the goods produced in the Northwest marketed? What role did this play in the pre-1860 sectional alignment?
31. What factors and inventions contributed to the growth and expansion of the Northwest's economy? Who were the men responsible for this?

IDENTIFICATION

Identify each of the following, and explain why it is important within the context of the chapter.

1. Supreme Order of the Star-Spangled Banner
2. Erie Canal
3. Mohawk and Hudson Railroad
4. Samuel F. B. Morse
5. merchant capitalists
6. Charles Goodyear
7. the Lowell Offering
8. Factory Girls Association
9. National Trades' Union
10. Commonwealth v. Hunt
11. Central Park
12. Mary Lyon
13. "female virtues"
14. John Deere
15. Cyrus H. McCormick

DOCUMENT 1

Few places better reflected the growth and diversity of the United States than the city of New York. With the opening of the Erie Canal, New York City became the gateway to the West, and its size grew with its importance. The following account of the city was written by James Silk Buckingham, an Englishman who visited America between 1837 and 1840. What impressed him most about the city? How did his English experience seem to shape these impressions? What evidence did Buckingham find of social customs and distinctions being different from those of Europe? What do you feel accounted for this?

What accounted for New York's growth and diversity? What forces combined to make it America's principal city? Considering the nationalistic spirit of the age, how would Americans have responded to Buckingham's description? Assuming that his assessment was accurate, would they have pointed with pride to the city? Why?

> The hotels are generally on a larger scale than in England. The great Astor House, which overlooks the Park from the west side of Broadway, is much larger in area than the largest hotels in London or Paris; it makes up 600 beds, and has a proportionate establishment to suit the scale of its general operations. It is built wholly of granite, is chaste in its style of architecture, and is called after the rich John Jacob Astor.

> Of places of public amusement there are a great number, including six theatres, which are well filled every night, though the majority of what would be called the more respectable classes of society, the most opulent, and the most religious members of the community do not generally patronize or approve of theatrical exhibitions under the present management.

> The private dwellings contain, as must be the case in all large cities, a great society of kinds and descriptions. The older houses are small, and most built of wood painted yellow or white. These are now confined to the residences of the poorer classes and are fast disappearing in every quarter, their places being occupied by substantial buildings of brick, though here and there are a few with granite fronts. The style of decoration, in the steps of ascent, the area of railings, and the doors, is more florid and ornamental than in the best parts of London, and the interior of the principal houses may be described as spacious, handsome, and luxurious, with lofty passages, good staircases, large rooms, and costly and gorgeous furniture. There are many individual houses of much greater splendour in London than any to be seen in New York, especially in the mansions of the English nobility; but, on the whole, the number of large, commodious, and elegantly furnished private dwellings in New York is much greater in proportion to the whole population than those in London, and approaches nearer to the ratio of Edinburgh or Paris.

> The streets are very unequal in their proportions and conditions. The great avenue of Broadway is striking from its continuous and unbroken length of three miles in a straight line; but its breadth, about eighty feet, is not sufficiently ample for the due proportion of its length. It is, moreover, wretchedly paved, both in the centre and on the sides. Large holes and deep pits are frequently seen in the former; and the latter, while before some houses the slabs of stone are large, uniform, and level, there is often an immediate transition from these to broken masses of loose stones, that require the greatest caution to pass over, especially in wet or frosty weather. The lighting and cleansing of the streets are not nearly so good as in the large towns of England, the gas being scanty in quantity, the lamps too far removed from each other, and the body of scavengers [garbage collectors] both weak in numbers and deficient in organizations. Some of the smaller streets are almost impassible in times of rain and snow; and, when not incommoded by a profusion of mud or water, they are prolific in their supply of dust. Many of the streets have trees planted along the edge of the foot pavement on each side, which in summer affords an agreeable shade, but in autumn it has the disagreeable effect of strewing the path with falling leaves, and in winter it makes the aspect more dreary.

A custom prevails, in the principal streets for shops, of having wooden pillars planted along the outer edge of the pavement, with horizontal beams reaching from pillar to pillar, not unlike the stanchions and crosspieces of a ropewalk. . . .

Broadway, which is greatly disfigured by these, is therefore much inferior to Regent Street in London in the general air of cleanliness, neatness, light, spaciousness, good pavement, and fine shops, by which the latter is characterized; and although the number of beautiful and gayly dressed ladies, who make Broadway their morning promenade, uniting shopping, visiting, and walking at the same time, gives it a very animated appearance of a fine day, between twelve and two o'clock, yet the absence of handsome equipages and fine horses, and the fewness of well-dressed gentlemen who have the leisure to devote to morning promenades of pleasure occasions Broadway to be inferior in the general effect of brilliance and elegance to the throng of Regent Street on a fine day in May, between three and four o'clock.

The population of New York is estimated at present to be little short of 300,000. Of these perhaps there are 20,000 foreigners, including English and persons from Canada and the British possessions, and 30,000 strangers from other states of the Union, making therefore the fixed resident population 250,000 and the floating population about 50,000 more. The greatest number of these are engaged in commerce or trade, with a due admixture of professional men, as clergy, physicians, and lawyers. But among them all there are fewer than perhaps in any other community in the world who live without any ostensible avocation. The richest capitalists still take a part in the business proceedings of the day; and men who have professedly retired and have no counting-house or mercantile establishment still retain so much of the relish for profitable occupation that they mingle freely with the merchants, and are constantly found to be the buyers and sellers of stock, in funds, or shares in companies, canals, railroads, banks, et cetera.

The result of all this is to produce the busiest community that any man could desire to live in. In the streets all is hurry and bustle; the very cars, instead of being drawn by horses at a walking pace, are often met at a gallop, and always in a brisk trot.

J. S. Buckingham, *America, Historical, Statistic, and Descriptive* (New York: Harper and Brothers, 1841), p. 42–46.

DOCUMENT 2

The growth of American industry was one of the more remarkable aspects of the pre-Civil War era, and the town and factory of Lowell, Massachusetts, became known as the finest example of what American ingenuity could accomplish. One of those impressed by what he found at Lowell was the frontiersman and folk hero David Crockett, who left the following account.

What impressed Crockett most about the factory at Lowell? How did what he witnessed differ from the economy of the section from which he came? What did Crockett see as the general benefit of an operation such as the one at Lowell? With which political party did his views seem most closely associated?

What gave rise to the "prejudices against these manufactories" Crockett mentions as being held by the West and the South? What was taking place at the time this was written (1834) that would ease the prejudices in the former and heighten them in the latter?

Next morning I rose early, and started for Lowell in a fine carriage, with three gentlemen who had agreed to accompany me. I had heard so much of this place that I longed to see it not because I had heard of the "miles of gals"; no, I left that for the gallantry of the president, who is admitted, on that score, to be abler than myself: but I wanted to see the power of the machinery, wielded by the keenest calculations of human skill; I wanted to see how it was that these northerners could buy our cotton, and carry it home, manufacture it, bring it back, and sell it for half nothing; and, in the mean time, be well to live, and make money besides. . . .

There are about fourteen thousand inhabitants [in Lowell]. It contains nine meeting houses; appropriates seven thousand five hundred dollars for free schools; provides instruction for twelve hundred scholars, daily; and about three thousand annually partake of its benefits. It communicates with Boston by the Middlesex canal (the first ever made in the United States); and in a short time the railroad to Boston will be completed, affording every facility the intercourse to the seaboard.

This place has grown by, and must depend on its manufactures. Its location renders it important, not only to the owners, but to the nation. Its consumption not only employs the thousands of its own population, but many thousands far away from them. It is calculated not only to give individual happiness and prosperity, but to add to our national wealth and independence; and instead of depending on foreign countries, to have our own material worked up in our own country. . . .

I never witnessed such a combination of industry, and perhaps never will again. I saw the whole process, from the time they put in the raw material, until it came out completely finished. In fact, it almost came up to the old story of a fellow walking into a patent machine with a bundle of wool under his arm, and coming out at the other end with a new coat on.

Nothing can be more agreeable than the attention that is paid by every one connected with these establishments. Nothing appears to be kept secret—every process is shown and with great cheerfulness. I regret that more of our southern and western men do not go there, as it would help much to do away with their prejudices against these manufactories.

David Crockett, *Life of David Crockett, The Original Humorist and Irrepressible Backwoodsman* (Philadelphia: Potter, 1865), pp. 213–317.

MAP EXERCISE

Fill in or identify the following on the blank maps provided. Use the maps on page 257 of the text as your source.

1. State boundaries.
2. Principal rivers.
3. Railroad routes in 1850.
4. Principal cities on the 1850 routes.
5. Railroad routes in 1860.
6. Principal cities on the 1860 routes.
7. Main East-West lines.

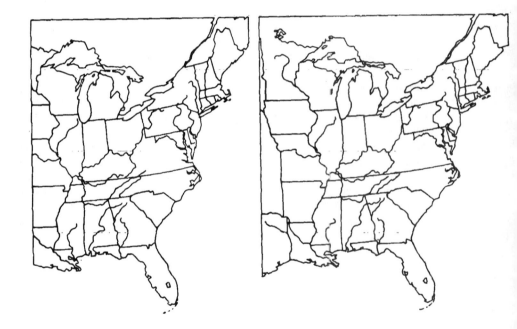

Interpretative Questions

Based on what you have filled in, answer the following. For some of the questions you will need to consult the narrative in your text for information or explanation.

1. Compare and contrast the 1850 and 1860 maps. Where did most of the railroad construction take place? How did this construction change earlier transportation patterns?

2. Where railroads went industry follcwed (and vice versa). What does the growth of railroads between 1850 and 1860 suggest about the industrial development of the ration?

3. Compare the principal cities in 1850 to those in 1860. Where were most of the rising urban centers located? What does this indicate about the economy and way of life in the North and the South?

4. Identify the railroad lines that linked North to South in 1850 and those that linked North to Scuth in 1860. What does this suggest about how this transportation network united or divided the nation?

SUMMARY

In the 1830s and 1840s the United States underwent an economic revolution. This was especially evident in the Nort, where the economy was characterized by industrial expansion, by the growth cf transportation systems (especially railroads), and by an increasingly diverse population. Cultural diversity produced uneasiness among some and a nativist movement appeared, while the gap between the rich and poor reflected an unequal distribution of wealth that disturbed some observers. But despite some labor unrest, there was little real class conflict, for where economic mobility might be lacking, geographic mobility often eased pressures. It was also in this era that the nature and the function of the family was changed by the forces of industrialization. Now many working-class women toiled in the mills, while their middle-class counterparts were assigned to the "female sphere" where their role in life was set out for them. In addition to the rapid expansion of business and industry in the region, the North also underwent agricultural changes that improved production and tied the Northeast economically to the Northwest.

CHAPTER SELF-TEST

After you have read the chapter in the text and done the exercises in the study guide, the following self-test can be taken to see if you understand the material you have covered. Answers appear at the end of the study guide.

Multiple Choice

Circle the letter of the response that best answers the question or completes the statement.

1. The American industrial revolution was the result of which of the following factors?
   a. Population growth
   b. Advances in transportation and communications
   c. The growth of manufacturing technology

d. a and

e. a and c

f. All of the above

2. One of the immediate results of the new transportation routes constructed during the "canal age" was:
   a. an increased white settlement in the Northwest.
   b. an increased white settlement in the Southwest.
   c. the renewed cooperation between states and the national government on internal improvement projects.
   d. the conviction that the national government should be responsible for all internal improvements.

3. During the 1820s and 1830s, railroads:
   a. played only a secondary role in the nation's transportation system.
   b. replaced canals as the most important means of transportation.
   c. generated little interest among American businessmen.
   d. consisted of a few long lines, which were not connected to water routes.

4. In the period covered by this chapter, most of the immigrants came from:
   a. England and Scotland.
   b. Ireland and Germany.
   c. Africa.
   d. Central Europe, especially Poland.

5. The most profound economic development in mid-nineteenth-century America was the:
   a. development of a national banking system.
   b. creation of corporations.
   c. decline of the small-town merchant and general store.
   d. rise of the factory.

6. The beginnings of an industrial labor supply can be traced to:
   a. overcrowding in American cities.
   b. a dramatic increase in food production.
   c. the use of slaves in manufacturing industries
   d. an increase in European immigration.

7. The Lowell or Waltham system of recruiting labor was to:
   a. enlist young women from farm families.
   b. recruit whole families from rural areas.

c. recruit newly arrived immigrants.

d. enlist young men from farm families.

8. The paternalistic factory system of Lowell and Waltham did not last long because:

a. workers resented being watched over so carefully.

b. in the highly competitive textile market, manufacturers were eager to cut labor costs.

c. unions undermined the owners' authority.

d. men found jobs in the factories, and they disliked the paternalistic system.

9. Most of the industrial growth experienced in the United States between 1840 and 1860 took place in:

a. the South and Southwest.

b. the Old Northwest.

c. the New England and the mid-Atlantic states.

d. Ohio Valley.

10. Which of the following was *not* a technological advance that sped the growth of industry during this period?

a. Better machine tools

b. Interchangeable parts

c. Improved water-power generators

d. New steam engines

11. The railroad network that developed during this period linked the:

a. the Northeast to the Northwest.

b. the Northeast to the Gulf Coast.

c. the east coast to the west coast.

d. New York to New Orleans.

12. Crucial to the operation of railroads was:

a. a system of federal railroad regulations.

b. the invention of the telegraph.

c. slave labor to build the lines.

d. a canal and river system that supported the lines.

13. Which of the following helped enlarge the urban population in this era?

a. Immigrants from Europe

b. Northeastern farmers

c. The growth of the population as a whole

d. All of the above

e. a and c

14. The nativist movement wanted to:
    a. return all land to Native Americans.
    b. enact more restrictive naturalization laws.
    c. increase aid to education so voters would be literate.
    d. make immigrants feel this was their home.

15. Which of the following did *not* inhibit the growth of effective labor resistance?
    a. Ethnic divisions between natives and immigrants.
    b. The availability of cheap labor.
    c. Slavery.
    d. The strength of the industrial capitalists.

16. Why did the unequal distribution of wealth not create more resentment?
    a. The actual living standard of the workers was improving.
    b. There was no social mobility, but people were content to stay where they were in the social system.
    c. Geographic mobility was limited, so there were few other opportunities.
    d. The political system offered few ways to express resentment.

17. In the middle-class family during this era, the role of women changed from:
    a. helpmate to workmate.
    b. "republican mother" to "democratic female."
    c. passive domestic to radical feminist.
    d. income producer to income consumer.

18. The growth of the agricultural economy of the Northwest affected the sectional alignment of the United States because:
    a. northwestern goods were sold to residents of the Northeast.
    b. northeastern industry sold its products to the Northwest.
    c. northwestern grain was sold to the South, which allowed it to grow more cotton.
    d. the Northwest was able to feed itself so it did not align with any other section.
    e. a and b
    f. a and d

True/False

Read each statement carefully. Mark true statements "T" and false statements "F."

___1. During the first half of the nineteenth century the United States grew more rapidly in population than Britain or Europe.

___2. During the first half of the nineteenth century the African-American population increased as fast or faster than the white population.

___3. The city which gained the most from the new transportation routes built in this era was New York.

___4. Railroads had so many advantages over canals that, where free competition existed, they almost always prevailed.

___5. Credit mechanisms in the early nineteenth century were well designed and efficient.

___6. When compared to working conditions in European industries, the Lowell mills were a paradise for working women.

___7. Artisans, displaced by the factory system, formed the first American labor unions.

___8. The most conspicuous change in American life in the 1840s and 1850s was the rapid industrialization of the Northeast.

___9. During this period international trade became increasingly important for the national economy.

___10. The South was an important part of the national railroad network.

___11. The majority of immigrants during this period came from Ireland and Russia.

___12. Although conditions got worse in American factories, few workers tried to do anything about it.

___13. Industrialization made no change in the nature and function of the American family.

___14. Except for teaching and nursing, work by women outside the household gradually came to be seen as a lower-class preserve.

___15. The typical white citizen of the Northwest was the owner of a reasonably prosperous family farm.

Review Questions

These questions are to be answered with essays. This will allow you to explore relationships among individuals, events, and attitudes of the period under review.

1. Examine the development of the system of roads and canals between 1815 and 1840. What geographical factors contributed to this? What sections did this transportation system link together, and what effect did the linkages have on the economies of the sections thus connected? How might this transportation network have influenced political alliances? In short, what effect did the system of canals and roads have on the nation as a whole?

2. How did the system of roads and canals in the previous question reflect the nationalistic thinking of Alexander Hamilton and Henry Clay? Consult earlier chapters in answering this question.

3. According to the text, "the most conspicuous change in American life in the 1840s and 1850s was the rapid industrialization of the Northeast." What changes occurred in this region during the period under consideration, and how did these changes tend to draw the Northeast and the Northwest more closely together economically, socially, and politically?

4. What impact did the economic changes in the North have on society there? Explain how industrialization affected labor, family life, and the role of women in the North.

CHAPTER ELEVEN

Cotton, Slavery, and the Old South

OBJECTIVES

A thorough study of Chapter 11 should enable you to understand:

1. The nature of the cotton economy in the antebellum South and how it influenced the region's commerce and industrial development.
2. The economic differences between the South and the North.
3. The structure of southern white society, and the role the various elements played in it.
4. The ways in which slavery could be both an economic and a social system.
5. What slavery was from the perspective of the slaveholder, the nonslaveholder, and the slave.
6. How and why some slaves resisted slavery, and how and why some seemed not to.
7. The "culture of slavery."

PERTINENT QUESTIONS

The Cotton Economy (pp. 282–287)

1. What was "the most important economic development in the South of the mid-nineteenth century"? What caused this, and what was its economic impact?
2. What role did the businessman of the South play in the region's economic development? What element was most important in this group? Why?
3. What elements were necessary for extensive industrial development? Did the South possess these? If not, why not?
4. What does the author mean by the statement that the antebellum South had a "colonial" economy?

Southern White Society (pp. 287–291)

5. What groups made up the planter aristocracy? Why did their influence far exceed their numbers?
6. What was the "cavalier" image, and how were southern planters able to create it?
7. How was the role played by affluent southern white women like that of their northern counterparts? How was it different?
8. What accounted for the difference identified in question 7? Why did so few southern white women rebel against their role?
9. If "the typical white southerner was not a great planter," what was he? Describe and explain the way of life of the southern "plain folk"—men and women.
10. Why did so few nonslaveholding whites oppose the slaveholding oligarchy? Where did these opponents live?

Slavery: The "Peculiar Institution" (pp. 291–298)

11. What were slave codes? What function did they serve? How were they applied, and what resulted from their violation?
12. How was slave life shaped by the slave's relationship with his or her owner?
13. To a slave, what was life under slavery?
14. Were there "classes" among the slaves? What evidence is there to support this?
15. How did slavery in cities differ from slavery on the plantation? What effect did urban slavery have on the "peculiar institution" and on the relationship between white and black?
16. What was life like for free blacks? How was freedom gained, and what were their opportunities once free?
17. How did slaves respond to slavery? What evidence exists to show that slaves did not accept their condition without protest and that, in some cases, they were strongly defiant?
18. What were the most widely recognized slave revolts? What effects did they have?

The Culture of Slavery (pp. 298–301)

19. What role did religion play in the life of slaves? How did slaves influence religion in America?
20. How were language and music important in the life of slaves?
21. What role did the family play in the life of slaves?
22. Explain the legal restrictions that were placed on slave families and on the religious life of slaves.

23. How has the debate over the nature of plantation slavery evolved from the abolitionists' interpretation before the Civil War up to the present? How have the various interpretations in this debate reflected the times in which they appeared?

IDENTIFICATION

Identify each of the following, and explain why it is important within the context of the chapter.

1. "upper South"
2. factors
3. *De Bow's Commercial Review*
4. George Fitzhugh
5. planters
6. "hill people"
7. "crackers"
8. southern chivalry
9. "pidgin"
10. household servants
11. "head driver"
12. Elizabeth Keckley
13. "Sambo" image
14. Gabriel Prosser
15. Nat Turner
16. "slave patrols"

DOCUMENT 1

In the South, the plantation dominated the economy, much as industry did in the Northeast. Following is a description of and some observations on the plantation system and slave labor taken from the travel account of Frederick Law Olmsted. What similarities do you find between the regimentation of the factory workers at Lowell and the status of the slaves? What differences exist? How did the objectives of the plantation owner differ from the objectives of those who owned the mills at Lowell? Might the plantation owner have argued that he offered his charges many of the same things as the factory? What analogy was the South fond of drawing between the factory and the plantation? What does this excerpt tell you about that analogy?

> It is difficult to handle simply as property, a creature possessing human passions and human feelings, however debased and torpid the condition of that creature may be; while, on the other hand, the absolute necessity of dealing with property as a thing, greatly embarrassed a man in any attempt to treat it as a person. And it is the natural

result of this complicated state of things, that the system of slave-management is irregular, ambiguous, and contradictory; that it is never either consistently humane or consistently economical.

As a general rule, the larger the body of negroes on a plantation or estate, the more completely they are treated as mere property, and in accordance with a policy calculated to insure the largest pecuniary returns. Hence, in part, the greater proportionate profit of such plantations, and the tendency which everywhere prevails in the planting districts to the absorption of small, and the augmentation of large estates. It may be true, that among the wealthier slave-owners there is oftener a humane disposition, a better judgement, and a greater ability to deal with their dependents indulgently and bountifully, but the effects of this disposition are chiefly felt, even on those plantations where the proprietor resides permanently, among the slaves employed about the house and stables, and perhaps a few old favourites in the quarters. It is more than balanced by the difficulty of acquiring a personal interest in the units of a large body of slaves, and an acquaintance with the individual characteristics of each. The treatment of the mass must be reduced to a system, the ruling idea of which will be, to enable one man to force into the same channel of labour the muscles of a large number of men in various and often conflicting wills.

Frederick Law Olmsted, *The Cotton Kingdom* (London: Sampson Low, Son, 1862), p. 192.

DOCUMENT 2

As the "Debating the Past" discussion on p. 330 indicates, slavery has been debated for some time. Following is an excerpt from Joseph B. Cobb's *Mississippi Scenes,* published in 1851, that sheds some light on the question of the slave's response to slavery. Read it, and consider how it relates to the information and points of view presented in the text. From it determine, at least in this case, how slavery apparently changed blacks, and what elements of the system brought these changes about. In studying this question, reexamine Document 1. Would you call slavery a brutal system or, as many southerners (including Joseph B. Cobb) contended, a "positive good"?

> The late Hon. William H. Crawford, so affectionately and proudly remembered by all Georgians, owned four native Africans, brought to this country among the last importations of those unfortunate wretches who could be sold within the time prescribed by the Federal Constitution. . . . In the same neighborhood, there happened to be residing another native African, rather more Americanized than the first, and these five old fellows. . . . were treated with marked respect by all the other negroes for miles and miles around. . . . Their illustrious owner himself always treated them with rather more kindness of manner and respect than his other slaves, and would never allow them to be subjected to the lash except in case of downright resistance to the authority of his overseer. . . . Their habits and dispositions were as unlike those of our native negroes as it is possible to conceive, when it is considered that they are of the same race. They had none of the merry-heartedness and vivacity. . . . of our Southern negroes, and though not decidedly morose, or fractious, they were yet exclusive, and somewhat unapproachable. They require far less whipping to coerce attention to their tasks. . . . On the other hand, our Southern negroes rarely ever resist.

. . . , but they are generally indolent and careless if they are allowed to think that whipping will not be resorted to. I never knew a native African to run away from his master's plantation. They stand their ground doggedly, like the Roman or British soldier, regardless of consequences; and to carry out the simile, they often fight with the same determined courage, unhappily for them!

Joseph B. Cobb, *Mississippi Scenes* (Philadelphia: Hart, 1851), pp. 173–174.

MAP EXERCISE

Fill in or identify the following on the blank maps provided. Use the maps on page 283 of the text as your source.

1. The slave states in 1820 and 1860.
2. The distribution of slavery and cotton production in 1820 and 1860.

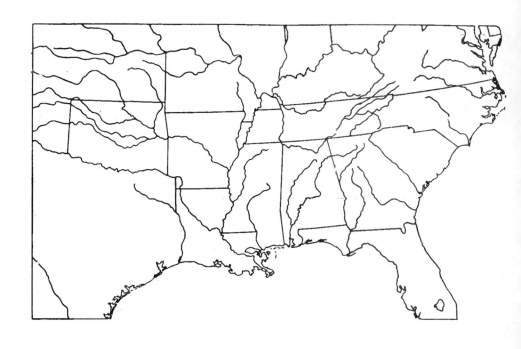

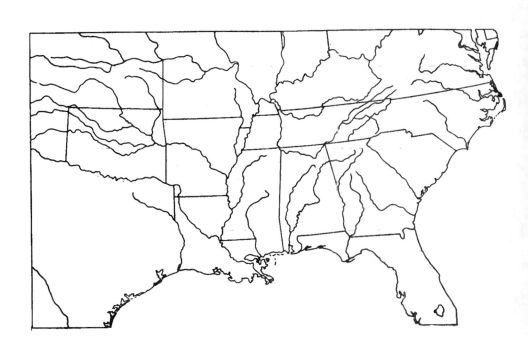

Interpretative Questions

Based on what you have filled in, answer the following. For some of the questions you will need to consult the narrative in your text for information or explanation.

1.   How did slavery relate to the growing of cotton? In what ways did slave labor serve the cotton economy, and how does this explain the relationship between the two?

2.   In what non-cotton-growing areas did slavery exist? What economic role did slavery play in these areas?

3.   Note the places where slavery did not exist. What was the economy of these areas? In what way did society in these areas differ from those areas where there was slavery?

SUMMARY

During the 1830s and 1840s economic power shifted from the "upper South" to the "lower South" and with this shift came a shift in political power as well. During this period antebellum southern society began to take on the features of what is popularly known as the "Old South." In the cotton kingdom planters and "plain folks," masters and slaves, plantation mistresses and farmers' wives coexisted, and together created a unique social order. Central to this structure was the region's "peculiar institution." More than just an economic system, slavery was a critical, creative force in the whole social order. Slaves contributed to white culture while creating a culture all their own. In the process they added to the complexity of a region that stood apart from the rest of the nation and seemed to pride itself in the differences.

CHAPTER SELF-TEST

After you have read the chapter in the text and done the exercises in the study guide, the following self-test can be taken to see if you understand the material you have covered. Answers appear at the end of the study guide.

Multiple Choice

Circle the letter of the response that best answers the question or completes the statement.

1.   The southern failure to create a flourishing commercial or industrial economy was in part the result of
   a.   a lack of business talent in the South.
   b.   an unwillingness on the part of southerners to take risks.

c. a set of values distinctive to the South that discouraged the growth of cities and industry.

d. a slave labor force that could not work successfully in industry.

2. A minority of southern whites owned slaves:
   a. and nonslaveholders dominated the political system in the region.
   b. but the slaveholding planters exercised power and influence far in excess of their numbers.
   c. so slavery was not very important in the lives of most whites.
   d. and most whites were happy with it that way.

3. In its efforts to develop industrially the South was hampered by:
   a. a rudimentary financial system.
   b. an inadequate transportation system.
   c. a "colonial dependency" on outside goods.
   d. All of the above

4. According to the "cavalier" myth, southern planters:
   a. were racially superior to common farmers.
   b. were chosen by God to dominate the South.
   c. were more concerned with a refined and gracious way of life than with industrial development.
   d. kept slaves even though it was unprofitable

5. Most southern white "ladies" were:
   a. less subordinate to men than in the North.
   b. relatively isolated from people outside their own families.
   c. better educated than their northern counterparts.
   d. more likely to engage in public activities or income-producing employment than their northern counterparts.

6. The typical white southerner was:
   a. a planter with many slaves and a lot of land.
   b. a small-town merchant or professional man.
   c. extremely poor.
   d. a modest yeoman farmer.

7. Which of the following was *not* a condition of slave life in the South?
   a. An adequate yet simple diet
   b. Hard work, even for women and children
   c. The freedom to use the time after work as they wished to
   d. Isolation and control

8. Slave women were:
   a. generally better treated than the men.
   b. not required to do household chores if they did field work.

c. frequently required to do field work as well as take care of families.

d. assigned mostly to household duties.

9. Free blacks were:
   a. seldom found in towns or cities
   b. mostly found in Virginia and Maryland.
   c. financially as well off as most poor whites.
   d. better off in the South than in the North.

10. The most important method of slave resistance was:
    a. everyday behavior by which blacks defied their masters.
    b. open rebellion.
    c. running away.
    d. arson.

11. Slave religion:
    a. differed little from the Christianity practiced by masters.
    b. rejected all African religious forms.
    c. offered a means for natural leaders to emerge.
    d. accepted the master's interpretation of the Bible.

12. Slave religious services:
    a. were restrained and unemotional.
    b. stressed a hope for freedom in this world, not the next.
    c. often spoke of resistance and rebellion.
    d. focused on salvation and not on worldly things.

13. Family life under slavery was:
    a. limited by legal restrictions.
    b. encouraged to keep the slaves happy.
    c. encouraged as a means of producing more slaves for the master.
    d. of little or no concern to masters.

14. Among slaves, family ties were:
    a. weak because marriages were not legal.
    b. easily maintained because masters tried to keep families together.
    c. very different from what we call the "nuclear family" today.
    d. generally no less strong than those of whites.

15. Religion influenced the resistance efforts of:
    a. Gabriel Prosser.
    b. Denmark Vesey.
    c. Nat Turner.
    d. All of the above.

True/False

Read each statement carefully. Mark true statements "T" and false statements "F."

___1.   The South, like the North, changed from an agricultural to an industrial economy during this period.

___2.   The new product that made cotton "king" in the South was short-staple cotton.

___3.   According to *De Bow's Commercial Review,* the South had a "colonial" relationship with the North.

___4.   Planters in the South were just as much competitive capitalists as the industrialists in the North.

___5.   Most whites who did not own slaves lived far from the planters and their plantations.

___6.   Most southern planters did not think of themselves as aristocrats.

___7.   There is little evidence that southern planters had sexual relations with their slaves.

___8.   Most whites who did not own slaves opposed slavery and resented the planter class.

___9.   Nonslaveholders had little contact with slaveholders.

___10.   Because of slavery, the South was very undemocratic.

___11.   About the same percentage of slaves could read and write as poor whites.

___12.   There is no evidence that any sort of paternal relationship ever existed between master and slave.

___13.   Masters encouraged slaves to accept Christianity because they believed it would make them accept their lot in life.

___14.   Slaves were generally more healthy than whites in the South.

___15.   The dominant response of African Americans to slavery was a combination of adaptation and resistance.

___16.   One of the most frequent causes of flight from the plantation was a slave's desire to find family members.

Review Questions

These questions are to be answered with essays. This will allow you to explore relationships among individuals, events, and attitudes of the period under review.

1.   What was "the southern way of life" for the white southerner? Be sure to look at more than the life of the planter.

2.   If nothing else, slavery set the South apart, made it unique. But how did the institution function, and what was its impact on the slave?

Analyze the plantation system—its social and its economic functions. How did it control its labor? And what was the response of these workers? How had this institution evolved since colonial times? (Be sure to consult previous chapters when answering this question.)

3. Compare and contrast the way of life of southern white women and black women during the 1840s and 1850s. How did the institution of slavery affect them both? How did the way of life of southern white women compare to that of women in the North? (Be sure to consult previous chapters when answering this question.)

4. What was slavery like for the slave? Examine the daily life of a slave—work, family life, diet, restrictions, and resistance.

5. What was the "culture of slavery"? How did slaves try to make their world a better place for themselves and their families?

CHAPTER TWELVE

An Age of Reforms

OBJECTIVES

A thorough study of Chapter 12 should enable you to understand:

1. The two basic impulses that were reflected in the reform movements, and examples of groups illustrating each impulse.
2. The transcendentalists and their place in American society.
3. The sources of American religious reform movements, why they originated where they did, their ultimate objectives, and what their leadership had in common.
4. The sources from which the philosophy of reform arose.
5. American educational reform in the antebellum period, and the contribution of education to the growth of nationalism.
6. The role of women in American society, and the attempts to alter their relationships with men.
7. The origins of the antislavery movement, the sources of its leadership, and how the movement in America fit into a world-wide antislavery effort.
8. The role of abolitionism in the antislavery movement, and the strengths and weaknesses of that part of the movement.

PERTINENT QUESTIONS

The Romantic Impulse (pp. 306–314)

1. How was the work of James Fenimore Cooper the culmination of an effort to produce a truly American literature? What did his work suggest about the nation and its people?
2. Why was Whitman called the "poet of American democracy"?
3. Who were the transcendentalists? What was their philosophy, and how did they express it in literature?
4. How did the transcendentalists attempt to apply their beliefs to the problems of everyday life at Brook Farm? What was the result?

5. How did the utopian communities attempt to redefine the sex roles? Which communities were most active in this effort, and what did they accomplish?
6. Who were the Mormons? What were their origins, what did they believe, and why did they end up in Utah?

Remaking Society (pp. 314–320)

7. The "philosophy of reform" that shaped this era rose from what two distinct sources?
8. What gave rise to the crusade against drunkenness? What successes and failures resulted from the movement's efforts?
9. How did efforts to produce a system of universal public education reflect the spirit of the age?
10. What were the problems facing public education, and what types of institutions were created to deal with them?
11. How did the rise of feminism reflect not only the participation of women in social crusades, but also a basic change in the nature of the family?
12. How did feminists benefit from their association with other reform movements—most notably, abolitionists—and at the same time suffer as a result?

The Crusade Against Slavery (pp. 320–327)

13. What was the antislavery philosophy of William Lloyd Garrison? How did he transform abolitionism into "a new and dramatically different phenomenon"?
14. What role did black abolitionists play in the movement? How did their philosophy compare with that of Garrison?
15. Why did many northern whites oppose the abolitionist movement? How did they show this opposition?
16. What efforts did abolitionists make to find political solutions to the question of slavery? How successful were they initially?
17. How did abolitionists attempt to arouse widespread public anger over slavery through the use of propaganda? What was the most significant work to emerge from this effort? Why did it have such an impact?

IDENTIFICATION

Identify each of the following, and explain why it is important within the context of the chapter.

1. Hudson River School
2. "Resistance to Civil Government'

3. Southern realists
4. *The Blithedale Romance*
5. "Owenites"
6. Shakers
7. Book of Mormon
8. Charles Grandison Finney
9. phrenology
10. Horace Mann
11. asylums
12. Seneca Falls convention
13. Sarah and Angelina Grimké
14. Catharine Beecher and Harriet Beecher Stowe
15. Elizabeth Cady Stanton
16. American Colonization Society
17. Monrovia
18. American Antislavery Society
19. Frederick Douglass
20. Elijah Lovejoy
21. *Prigg* v. *Pennsylvania*
22. personal liberty laws

DOCUMENT

At the women's rights convention held at Seneca Falls, New York in 1848, the delegates declared that "all men and women are created equal" and listed the "injuries and usurpations on the part of man toward woman." Then the convention adopted a series of resolutions for constructive action, among which were the following. What do these tell you about the goals of the early women's rights movement? What do they also tell you about the prejudices that women would have to overcome to gain the equality they sought?

> *Resolved,* That the same amount of virtue, delicacy, and refinement of behavior that is required of woman in the social state, should also be required of man, and the same transgressions should be visited with equal severity on both man and woman.

> *Resolved,* That the objection of indelicacy and impropriety, which is so often brought against woman when she addresses a public audience, comes with a very ill grace from those who encourage, by their attendance, her appearance on the stage, in the concert, or in feats of the circus.

> *Resolved,* That it is the duty of the women of this country to secure to themselves their sacred right to the elective franchise.

> *Resolved,* That the equality of human rights results necessarily from the fact of the identity of the race in capabilities and responsibilities.

> *Resolved,* That the speedy success of our cause depends upon the zealous and untiring efforts of both men and women, for the overthrow of the monopoly of the pulpit, and

for the securing to women an equal participation in the various trades, professions, and commerce.

SUMMARY

By the 1820s, America was caught up in the spirit of a new age, and Americans, who had never been shy in proclaiming their nation's promise and potential, concluded that the time for action had come. Excited by the nation's technological advances and territorial expansions, many set as their goal the creation of a society worthy to be part of it all. What resulted was an outpouring of reform movements the likes of which had not been seen before and have not been seen since. Unrestrained by entrenched conservative institutions and attitudes, these reformers attacked society's ills wherever they found them, producing in the process a list of evils so long that many were convinced that a complete reorganization of society was necessary. Most, however, were content to concentrate on their own particular cause, and thus, at least at first, the movements were many and varied. But in time, most reformers seemed to focus on one evil that stood out above the rest. The "peculiar institution," slavery, denied all they stood for—equality, opportunity, and, above all, freedom. Slavery became the supreme cause.

CHAPTER SELF-TEST

After you have read the chapter in the text and done the exercises in the study guide, the following self-test can be taken to see if you understand the material you have covered. Answers appear at the end of the study guide.

Multiple Choice

Circle the letter of the response that best answers the question or completes the statement.

1. The reform movements of the first half of the nineteenth century reflected which of the following impulses?
   a. An optimistic faith in human nature
   b. A rational view of man and his ability
   c. A desire for control and order
   d. a and c

2. The first great American novelist was:
   a. Walt Whitman.
   b. James Fenimore Cooper.
   c. Herman Melville.
   d. Ralph Waldo Emerson.

3. Transcendentalists believed that:
   a. "understanding" was more important than "reason."
   b. man should repress instinct and strive for externally imposed learning.
   c. each individual should strive to "transcend" the limits of intellect and allow emotions to create an "original relation to the universe."
   d. individuals should avoid anything that would bring one too close to the natural world.

4. The Oneida Community:
   a. advocated "free love" to redefine gender roles.
   b. called for celibacy and attracted members for conversion.
   c. believed it liberated women from the demands of male "lust" and from traditional bonds of family.
   d. was widely accepted and had almost no critics.

5. Like other experiments in social organization of this era, Mormonism reflected:
   a. a strong antislavery bias.
   b. a celebration of individual liberty.
   c. a desire to improve the status of women.
   d. a belief in human perfectibility.

6. Evangelical Protestantism added major strength to which of the following reforms:
   a. Temperance
   b. Education and rehabilitation
   c. Women's rights
   d. Peace

7. During the early nineteenth century the practice of medicine was:
   a. unregulated and often the occupation of quacks.
   b. undertaken only by highly trained physicians.
   c. regulated by state and local government.
   d. regulated by professional organizations.

8. As women in various reform movements confronted the problems they faced in a male-dominated society, they responded by:
   a. withdrawing from the movements.
   b. accepting the notion that men and women were assigned separate "spheres" in society.
   c. focusing their attention on religious matters.
   d. setting in motion the first important feminist movement.

9. Which of the following groups was most involved in the feminist movement?
   a. Baptist
   b. Quakers
   c. Mormons
   d. Shakers

10. After 1830, which of the following reform movements began to overshadow the others?
   a. Antislavery
   b. Women's rights
   c. Temperance
   d. Education

11. The most noted black abolitionist of the day was:
   a. Ralph Waldo Emerson.
   b. William Lloyd Garrison.
   c. Frederick Douglass.
   d. Joseph Smith.

12. Opponents of abolitionism in the North believed:
   a. abolitionists were dangerous radicals.
   b. the movement would lead to a war between North and South.
   c. the movement would lead to a great influx of free blacks into the North.
   d. All of the above

13. "Immediate abolition gradually accomplished" was the slogan of:
   a. moderate antislavery forces.
   b. Garrison and his followers.
   c. antislavery southern planters.
   d. black abolitionists.

14. Personal liberty laws:
   a. allowed masters to claim slaves who ran away to the North.
   b. freed slaves who escaped to states in the Old Northwest.
   c. forbade state officials to assist in the capture and return of runaways.
   d. outlawed the interstate slave trade.

15. The movement that advocated keeping slavery out of the territories was known as the:
   a. "personal liberty" movement.
   b. "free soil" movement.
   c. John Brown Brigade.
   d. Garrison solution.

True/False

Read each statement carefully. Mark true statements "T" and false statements "F."

___1. American intellectuals were pleased with the high regard in which their culture was held by Europeans.

___2. Thoreau believed that a government that required an individual to violate his or her own morality had no legitimate authority.

___3. Because transcendentalism was at heart an individualistic philosophy, its followers did not take part in communal living experiments.

___4. The philosophy of reform in America drew heavily from Protestant revivalism.

___5. At the beginning of the Civil War, the United States had one of the highest literacy rates in the world.

___6. The idea of asylums for social deviants was not simply an effort to curb the abuses of the old system, but also an attempt to reform and rehabilitate the inmates.

___7. Early feminists made their point by drawing a parallel between the plight of women and the plight of slaves.

___8. The American Colonization Society failed because it challenged both property rights and southern sensibilities.

___9. The man who transformed the antislavery movement was Ralph Waldo Emerson.

___10. Although there was opposition to abolitionism in the North, it was generally peaceful.

___11. Radical abolitionists attacked slavery and the Constitution that seemed to sanction it.

___12. Abolitionists were also pacifists, and therefore did not advocate violence to free the slaves.

___13. Antislavery and abolition were different words for the same thing.

___14. Although it sold well, the novel *Uncle Tom's Cabin* had little impact on American antislavery attitudes.

___15. Only a relatively small number of people before the Civil War ever accepted the abolitionist position that slavery must be entirely eliminated in a single stroke.

Review Questions

These questions are to be answered with essays. This will allow you to explore relationships among individuals, events and attitudes of the period under review.

1. During this period, how did American intellectuals create a national culture committed to the liberation of the human spirit? How did their efforts relate to the efforts of social reformers?
2. What role did religion and religious leaders play in the reform movement described in this chapter? How did this differ from the role religion previously played in dealing with social issues? (Consult previous chapters when answering this question.)
3. Who were the major critics of slavery? On what grounds did they attack the institution, and what means to end it did they propose?
4. How did the reform movement affect the status of women? What role did women play in these efforts to change society, and what were they able to accomplish? (Be sure to consult previous chapters to understand the change taking place.)

CHAPTER THIRTEEN

The Impending Crisis

OBJECTIVES

A thorough study of Chapter 13 should enable you to understand:

1. Manifest Destiny, and America's westward migration into Texas, California, and Oregon.
2. The origin of the Republic of Texas, and the controversy concerning its annexation by the United States.
3. The reasons why the United States declared war on Mexico, and how the Mexican War was fought to a successful conclusion.
4. The impact of the Wilmot Proviso on the sectional controversy.
5. The methods used to enact the Compromise of 1850, and its reception by the American people.
6. The role of the major political parties in the widening sectional split.
7. The enactment of the Kansas-Nebraska Act, and the effect of this act on the attitudes of the people in all sections.
8. The impact of the *Dred Scott* decision on sectional attitudes and on the prestige of the Supreme Court.
9. The reasons for Abraham Lincoln's victory in 1860, and the effect of his election on this sectional crisis.

PERTINENT QUESTIONS

Looking Westward (pp. 331–336)

1. What was Manifest Destiny? What forces created this concept?
2. What was the "empire of liberty"? How was it to be achieved, and what doubts were raised about its desirability?
3. How did Texas become available for annexation? What prevented its immediate annexation?
4. What was the history of American interest in Oregon?
5. What were the characteristics of western migrants? What problems did they face? How were these overcome?

134

Expansion and War (pp. 336–342)

6. How did Polk's campaign catch the spirit of the time? What effect did Clay's position on Texas have on his campaign in the presidential election?
7. What were the goals of President Polk? How did he resolve the Oregon question?
8. What tensions emerged in the Southwest that threatened to lead the United States into war with Mexico?
9. How did American interest in California develop?
10. On what grounds did Polk ask Congress to declare war on Mexico?
11. On what grounds was Polk's call for war criticized?
12. What was Polk's plan for the conduct of the war?
13. What were the objectives of the American offensives in the war? What did they accomplish? What were the terms of the Treaty of Guadalupe Hidalgo?

The Sectional Debate (pp. 342–346)

14. What was the Wilmot Proviso? What brought about its introduction, and what arguments were advanced in its favor?
15. What were the South's arguments against the Wilmot Proviso? On what points did they differ from the arguments of the North?
16. How did the gold rush change the cultural composition of California?
17. What problems faced President Zachary Taylor when he took office? How did he propose to solve them, and what action did Congress initially take?
18. What was the Compromise of 1850? How was it passed?
19. Who were the "younger" politicians who emerged after 1850? How did they differ from the leaders they replaced?
20. How did the Compromise of 1850 differ from the Missouri Compromise?

The Crises of the 1850s (pp. 347–351)

21. How did the political parties react to the Compromise of 1850?
22. How did the sections of the country react to the Compromise of 1850?
23. What was the "Young America" movement? What national sentiment did it reflect? Who were its spokespersons? What did it accomplish?
24. How did the issue of a transcontinental railroad help to reopen the sectional controversy? Explain.

25. How did the North react to the Kansas-Nebraska Act? The South? What effect did it have on the Whigs? The Democrats?

26. Who were the Republicans? What caused their formation? Which groups composed this party, and what was the party's platform?

27. What problems were faced in the attempt to organize a legitimate government in Kansas? Why did these problems arise? How was it that Kansas became a battleground for the sectional controversy?

28. Explain the maneuvering by pro-slavery and antislavery forces to gain control of the Kansas government. What did both sides come to believe that Kansas symbolized for the nation?

29. What type of society did northerners wish to create? How did "free soil" and "free labor" fit into their plans? Why did they feel that the South was holding them back?

30. How did the "free-soil" ideology manifest itself in the Republican Party? What diverse views did it unite?

31. What were the elements of the South's pro-slavery response? Who were its major spokespersons?

32. How did southerners attempt to silence their opponents?

33. What effect did the depression of 1857 have on political divisions in America? How did it increase the tension between the North and the South? What did both sides see as the significance of this economic decline?

34. What were the origins of the *Dred Scott* case? What issues were involved, and what decision was handed down by the Court? How did the reaction to this case add to sectional tensions?

35. How did President James Buchanan respond to the Kansas question? What were his reasons, and what was the outcome? What does this tell you about the possibility of compromise on the issue of slavery in the territories?

36. Why did the Lincoln-Douglas debates take place, and why did they draw so much attention? How did Lincoln and Douglas differ on their solution to the question of slavery in the territories?

37. What were the goals of John Brown's raid, and why did it have such an impact on the South?

38. What caused the split between northern and southern Democrats in 1860, and what was the result of this division?

39. What was the Republican platform in 1860? To what specific political groups were the Republicans trying to appeal, and how did this platform propose to appeal to them?

IDENTIFICATION

Identify each of the following, and explain why it is important within the context of the chapter.

1. "penny press"
2. San Jacinto
3. Council Bluff
4. "Fifty-four forty or fight!"
5. the Nueces River
6. General Winfield Scott
7. Nicholas Trist
8. "All Mexico!"
9. Free-Soil Party
10. "Forty-niners"
11. Millard Fillmore
12. Jefferson Davis
13. Franklin Pierce
14. Anti-Nebraska Democrats
15. Stephen A. Douglas
16. Ostend Manifesto
17. Gadsden Purchase
18. Pottawatomie Massacre
19. Preston Brooks
20. free-soil ideology
21. "slave power conspiracy"
22. Uncle Tom's Cabin
23. John C. Breckenridge
24. Harper's Ferry

DOCUMENT 1

Below is an excerpt from a statement made in 1837 by John C. Calhoun that outlines his views on slavery. Note his comparison of the lot of slaves with that of European (and northern?) workers. How might William Lloyd Garrison have responded to this?

> I hold that in the present state of civilization, where two races of different origin, and distinguished by color, and other physical differences, as well as intellectual, are brought together, the relation now existing in the slaveholding States between the two is, instead of an evil, a good—a positive good. I feel myself called upon to speak freely upon the subject where the honor and interests of those I represent are involved. I hold then, that there never has yet existed a wealthy and civilized society

in which one portion of the community did not, in point of fact, live on the labor of the other. . . . I may say with truth that in few countries so much is left to the share of the laborer, and so little exacted from him, or where there is more kind attention paid to him in sickness or infirmities of age. Compare his condition with the tenants of the poor houses in the more civilized portions of Europe—look at the sick and the old and infirm slave, on one hand, in the midst of his family and friends, under the kind superintending care of his master and mistress, and compare it with the forlorn and wretched condition of the pauper in the poor house.

DOCUMENT 2

One of the most outspoken critics of the Mexican War was the Massachusetts poet James Russell Lowell. Like so many of his fellow New Englanders, he believed that the conflict was part of an effort to advance the interests of the South, a view he set forth in The *Bigelow Papers,* a collection of observations that Lowell attributed to one Hosea Bigelow. In the following poem, Bigelow confronts a recruiting sergeant and explains, in Yankee vernacular, his opposition to the war.

What does Bigelow see as the main purpose of the war with Mexico? Whom does he blame, and why? What role does he see the North playing in the war, and what does he feel the results will be? Look at the final verse. What solution does he propose? Remember this when we get to 1860. With such sentiments being expressed in the North, why will the northern states be willing to fight to preserve the Union?

'T would n't suit them Southern fellers,
  They're a dreffle graspin' set,
We must ollers blow the bellers
  Wen they want their irons het;

May be its all right ez preachin'
  By *my* narves it kind o' grates,
Wen I see the overreachin'
  O' them nigger-drivin' States.

They may talk o' Freedom's airy
  Tell they're pupple in the face,
It's a grand gret cemetary
  Fer the barthrights of our race;
They jest want this Californy
  So's to lug new slave-states in
To abuse ye, an' to scorn ye,
  An' to plunder ye like sin.

Aint it cute to see a Yankee
  Take sech everlastin' pains
All to git the Devil's thankee,
  Helpin' on 'em weld their chains?

Wy, it's jest ez clear ez figgers,
    Clear ez one an' one make two,
Chaps thet make black slaves o' niggers
    Want to make wite slaves o' you.

Ef I'd *my* way I hed ruther
    We should go to work an' part—
They take one way, we take t'other,—
    Guess it would n't break my heart;
Men hed ough' to put asunder
    Them thet God has noways jined,
An'.I should n't gretly wonder
    Ef there's thousands o' my mind.

James Russell Lowell, *The Bigelow Papers* (London: Trubner, 1859), pp. 4–9.

MAP EXERCISE

Fill in or identify the following on the blank map provided. Use the map on page 346 of the text as your source.

1. Free states and territories.
2. Slave states and territories (with slave percentages of total population).
3. Areas where the decision on slavery was left to the territories.
4. Missouri Compromise line.
5. District of Columbia.

Interpretative Questions

Based on what you have filled in, answer the following. For some of the questions you will need to consult the narrative in your text for information or explanation.

1. Study the areas that remained open to slavery. As far as the expansion of the institution is concerned, did the South gain or lose from the Compromise of 1850?
2. After studying the map, what evidence do you find to support John C. Calhoun's fear that the South would be relegated to permanent minority status?
3. How had the knowledge of land west of the Mississippi River changed since the early 1800s, and what impact did this have on settlement patterns? In the light of these changes, how would the population be expected to expand in the next few decades and what impact would this have on the balance between slave and free states in the Senate?
4. What changes did the Kansas-Nebraska Act make in the agreements reached in the Missouri Compromise and the Compromise of 1850?

SUMMARY

Between 1845 and 1860, critical events and issues seemed to come in a rush, giving Americans little time to analyze what was happening and reflect on long-range solutions. Emotion seemed to replace reason as the debate grew increasingly repetitive and loud. The question, or so it seemed, was the expansion of slavery into the territories gained during the Polk administration. But something far more fundamental was at stake—the future of the nation. Northerners had become convinced that the expansion of slavery threatened the democratic foundations of the United States and that expansion would give the South control of the government that would lead to economic stagnation, unemployment, and financial ruin—all the effect of the depression of 1837, but magnified. From this point of view, the South, and its "peculiar institution," threatened the nation's growth and progress and had to be overcome. The South, however, convinced of the legality of its position and the validity of its institutions, fought back, and with remarkable success. By combining the power in the Democratic Party (which gave it extraordinary influence in Congress and with the president) with its supporters on the Supreme Court, the slave states seemed secure. But still they were fearful. Convinced that they had given up all they could in earlier compromises, they feared future gains by those they considered to be enemies; and those they feared most were the Republicans.

CHAPTER SELF-TEST

After you have read the chapter in the text and done the exercises in the study guide, the following self-test can be taken to see if you understand the material you have covered. Answers appear at the end of the study guide.

Multiple Choice

Circle the letter of the response that best answers the question or completes the statement.

1. The idea that God and history had selected America to expand its boundaries over the continent of North America was known as:
    a. Manifest Destiny.
    b. divine right.
    c. white supremacy.
    d. nativism.

2. When the new republic of Texas requested annexation by the United States:
    a. the American government quickly agreed.
    b. Americans in the North opposed acquiring a large new slave territory.
    c. southerners, led by President Jackson, pushed for annexation.
    d. Mexico gave up all claims to Texas.

3. Which of the following was *not* part of President Polk's policy regarding New Mexico and California?
    a. Sending troops to the Nueces River in Texas
    b. Informing Americans in California that the United States would respond sympathetically to a revolt against Mexico
    c. Instructing the Pacific naval commander to seize California ports if Mexico declared war
    d. Ceasing all diplomatic contact with Mexico

4. By combining the Oregon and the Texas issue in 1844, Democrats hoped to:
    a. start a war with Mexico and Great Britain.
    b. attract John Tyler to the Democratic Party.
    c. divert attention from the slavery issue.
    d. appeal to both northern and southern expansionists.

5. The war with Mexico was criticized:
   a. by southerners who believed Polk deliberately maneuvered the country into the conflict on behalf of northern interests.
   b. by northerners who believed it was part of a slaveholders' plot to bring in more slave states.
   c. by businessmen who believed it would hurt commerce with England and Mexico.
   d. None of the above.

6. The Wilmot Proviso:
   a. went into law without the president's signature.
   b. passed the House but not the Senate.
   c. was a compromise acceptable to the South and the North but not the West.
   d. drew very little attention outside of Congress.

7. The Compromise of 1850 included all of the following except the proviso that:
   a. California would come in as a free state.
   b. in the rest of the lands acquired from Mexico, territorial governments would be formed without restrictions on slavery.
   c. the national government would not pay the Texas debt.
   d. the slave trade, but not slavery, would be abolished in the District of Columbia.

8. The new leaders emerging in Congress after the Compromise of 1850 were:
   a. less able politicians.
   b. more concerned with narrow interests of self-promotion.
   c. as skilled at compromise as the older leaders.
   d. interested in broad national issues.

9. The question of statehood for Kansas and Nebraska became a critical issue because:
   a. of the question of whether they would be slave or free states.
   b. of southern fear that a transcontinental railroad would be built through them.
   c. of northern concern over new wheat states and depressed grain prices.
   d. many believed that they could never support a population sufficient to justify statehood.

10. Northerners who accepted the concepts of "free soil" and "free labor" believed:
    a. slavery was dangerous not because of what it did to blacks but because of what it did to whites.
    b. slavery opened the door to economic opportunity for whites.
    c. slavery was what made the South a glorious civilization and one that should be admired.
    d. slave labor would work in northern factories and should be allowed to expand.

11. Southerners who believed in the 'positive good" theory argued:
    a. slavery was good for blacks.
    b. slavery was maintained, even though it was not profitable for whites.
    c. northern factory workers were better off than slaves, but they deserved to be better off because they were white.
    d. blacks were not biologically inferior, they just needed time to catch up culturally.

12. The *Dred Scott* decision:
    a. affirmed the South's argument that the Constitution guaranteed the existence of slavery.
    b. was a victory for the antislavery movement.
    c. declared Scott a free man.
    d. outlawed the interstate slave trade.

13. Abraham Lincoln:
    a. believed slavery was morally wrong but was not an abolitionist.
    b. had been a Democrat before he became a Republican.
    c. believed the expansion of slavery would hurt the spread of free labor.
    d. tried to avoid the slavery issue in his debates with Douglas.
    e. a and c
    f. a and d

14. The single event that did the most to convince white southerners they could not live safely in the Union was:
    a. the election of Lincoln.
    b. the Pottawatomie Massacre.
    c. John Brown's raid.
    d. the *Dred Scott* decision.

True/False

Read each statement carefully. Mark true statements "T" and false statements "F."

___1. The "penny press" was important because it exposed a significant proportion of the population to the rhetoric of nationalistic politicians.

___2. Indian attack was the greatest danger westward migrants faced.

___3. Texas was not able to get any European nation to recognize it as an independent nation.

___4. Though a "dark horse" candidate, James K. Polk was not an obscure politician.

___5. The Oregon question was finally settled by Britain surrendering claims below the 54th parallel.

___6. The United States did not take all of Mexico because its invasion of that country was not successful.

___7. The Wilmot Proviso prohibited slavery in the territory taken from Mexico.

___8. The South supported Taylor because he was a southerner and a slaveholder.

___9. The Compromise of 1850 passed, despite the opposition of Webster and Calhoun.

___10. After 1850 the Whig Party emerged as the one party without sectional divisions.

___11. The Kansas-Nebraska Act repealed the antislavery provision of the Missouri Compromise.

___12. Northerners saw Preston Brooks's attack on Charles Sumner as an example of the barbarism of the South, while southerners believed Sumner had insulted Brooks's uncle and got what he deserved.

___13. Northerners saw the "gag rule" as evidence of the "slave power conspiracy" against their liberties.

___14. President Buchanan proved a firm and decisive president at the very time the nation needed one.

___15. The Republican Party became the party of the "free-soil/free-labor" ideology.

___16. With Lincoln's election, the Republicans controlled both the legislative and the executive branches of the government.

Review Questions

These questions are to be answered with essays. This will allow you to explore relationships among individuals, events, and attitudes of the period under review.

1. What was the concept of Manifest Destiny and how did it influence American expansion west of the Mississippi River? What impact did this concept have on American foreign policy during this period? How is this concept rooted in the American colonial experience, especially that of New England? (See previous chapters in answering this question.)

2. Why did the South perceive the Wilmot Proviso as such a threat? What did the proviso indicate about the North's attitude toward slavery? Was the abolition of slavery the issue, or was it something else? Examine the proviso, its implications, and the southern response.

3. Eventually the majority of northerners came to believe that the existence of slavery was dangerous not because of what it did to blacks but because of what it threatened to do to whites. How did this feeling shape the northern attack on slavery, and how did southerners attempt to defend their institution?

4. Kansas became a symbol for both the North and the South—but a symbol of what? What did both sides find in the controversy over Kansas to support their charges against their adversaries? What did Kansas come to mean to the nation? Assess Kansas as a symbol of the positions and problems that characterized the divisions in the United States.

5. One historian has claimed that a lack of leadership contributed to the inability of the nation to overcome its divisions. This argument contends that a "blundering generation" of politicians who failed to understand the nature of the divisions offered solutions that resolved issues but did not deal with the real problems. Look at the concerns expressed by both the North and the South, and look at the proposals advanced to ease these concerns. From this assessment, do you feel that the "blundering generation" theory has merit, or were these deeper, fundamental questions that even the most capable leaders could not have resolved? In short, had the conflict between North and South become "irrepressible"?

CHAPTER FOURTEEN

The Civil War

OBJECTIVES

A thorough study of Chapter 14 should enable you to understand:

1. The reasons why all attempts to reach a compromise in the time-honored way failed in 1860 and 1861.
2. The unique problems faced by the newly inaugurated President Lincoln, and his use of executive powers to solve them up to July 4, 1861.
3. The ways in which the Confederate States of America compared with the United States in manpower, natural resources, finances, industrial potential, and public support.
4. The significant legislation enacted by Congress once Southern members were no longer a factor.
5. The considerations involved in President Lincoln's decision to issue the Emancipation Proclamation, and its reception in the North, in the South, and in Europe.
6. The basic structure of the government of the Confederate States of America, how it differed from that of the United States, and how it dealt with the vital question of states' rights.
7. The efforts of Presidents Lincoln and Davis to act as commander in chief under their respective constitutions.
8. How other nations, particularly England and France, viewed the struggle, and how their courses of action affected the outcome.
9. How the American Civil War fits into the worldwide movement to create large, consolidated nations.

PERTINENT QUESTIONS

The Secession Crisis (pp. 361–365)

1. Which states were the first to secede, and what was the reaction of the United States government to this?
2. What compromises were proposed to bring these states back into the Union, and why did they fail?

3. What was Abraham Lincoln's opinion on the legality of secession, and how was that opinion reflected in his action concerning Fort Sumter?
4. What advantages did the Union have in the Civil War? What were the advantages of the Confederacy?

The Mobilization of the North (pp. 365–370)

5. How did the Republican Party act to expand the American economy during the war? To which prewar party was their program similar? Why were they able to enact it, whereas the previous party was unable to do so?
6. How did the Union propose to finance the war? How successful was this? What was the effect on the economy?
7. How did the Union propose to raise troops? To what extent was it forced to use conscription? What was the reaction to this, and why was it so varied?
8. What were the characteristics of Lincoln as a leader? How were these characteristics reflected in his selection of his cabinet?
9. What was Lincoln's view of the extent of presidential war powers? Who were the opponents of the war, and how did Lincoln use these powers against them?
10. For what reason was the "Union Party" created? Who were its candidates?
11. What two factions were trying to control the Republican Party and what were the goals of each? Which faction did Lincoln support?
12. How was this split in the Republican Party revealed in the debate over what to do about slavery? What action did each faction propose? What did Lincoln do, and why?
13. What factors, other than political pressure, brought about the Emancipation Proclamation? What did the proclamation really accomplish? When did full emancipation really come?
14. What contributions did African Americans make to the Northern war effort? How did their treatment reflect the general racial attitudes of white America?
15. What impact did the Civil War have on women in the North?
16. What part did women play in the Union's war effort?

The Mobilization of the South (pp. 370–375)

17. Explain the origins of the Confederate government. How did its constitution differ from that of the United States? Who were chosen as its leaders, and what problems did they face?

18. How did the Confederacy attempt to finance the war? What problems did it face, and what were the results?

19. How did the Confederacy propose to raise troops for the war? How did these plans compare with those of the Union, and how successful were they? Why?

20. Why was states' rights the greatest source of division in the Confederacy's war effort? What caused this division, and what was the effect?

21. How did the Civil War "transform" Southern society? How was this transformation like that which took place in the North? How was it different?

22. How did the American Civil War fit into the worldwide movement to create large, consolidated nations?

Strategy and Diplomacy (pp. 375–380)

23. Compare and contrast Abraham Lincoln and Jefferson Davis—their backgrounds, abilities, and objectives. Why was Lincoln more successful at organizing a command system than Davis?

24. What role did Lincoln propose for the United States Navy? How did the Confederacy attempt to overcome this naval advantage and what was the result?

25. What were the foreign-policy objectives of the Union and the Confederacy? How did each attempt to achieve these objectives, which was most successful, and why?

Campaigns and Battles (pp. 380–394)

26. Explain the impact that technology had on the conduct of the war. Which technological inventions made the most difference and which side gained the most from their use?

27. What major engagements were fought in 1861? What did they reveal about the possibility of an early end to the struggle and about the readiness of the two sides for a major conflict?

28. What was the Union plan for the conquest of the West? How did the Confederates propose to defend this area? How did the campaign advance, what battles took place, and which of the two armies more nearly achieved its objectives?

29. What was the Union plan on the Virginia front in 1862? Who was the general selected to carry this out? Who was the Confederate

general he faced, and what was the relative strength of the two armies?

30. Outline the battles fought in the East in 1862. How did Lincoln's action toward his commanders affect the war effort? What were the relative positions of the two armies at the end of 1862? Which side had been more successful in achieving its objectives?

31. Why was 1863 the "year of decision"? What took place in 1863 to swing the advantage to the side of the Union? Where did these battles occur? Who were the generals involved? What did the battles accomplish? Why were they so important?

32. What was Grant's grand strategy for 1864? Who was to be in charge of the armies involved, and what were their objectives?

33. How was the Confederacy finally defeated? In what way did the Union forces destroy the South's will to carry on the fight?

34. How has the scholarly debate over the causes of the Civil War revolved around the question of whether it was a "repressible" or an "irrepressible" conflict?

IDENTIFICATION

Identify each of the following, and explain why it is important within the context of the chapter.

1. Maj. Robert Anderson
2. Crittenden Compromise
3. Homestead Act
4. Morrill Land Grant Act
5. greenbacks
6. Copperheads
7. Joseph Brown and Zebulon M. Vance
8. *Monitor* and *Merrimack* (Virginia)
9. *Trent* affair
10. The Emancipation Proclamation

Where did each of the following battles occur? Who was the victor, and what was the significance of the outcome?

1. First Bull Run
2. Shiloh
3. Murfreesboro
4. Seven Days
5. Second Bull Run
6. Antietam

DOCUMENT

Daniel O'Leary, a captain in the Union army, took part in the bloody fighting of the Chattanooga and Atlanta campaigns, and by the fall of 1864 had seen all of the war that he wanted to see. Having lost a brother fighting for the Union in Virginia and a brother-in-law, who fell in Dallas, Georgia, fighting for the Confederacy, he had every reason to feel tired and perhaps a bit disillusioned. The following is from a letter that he wrote to his wife just after his regiment had withdrawn from Atlanta and returned to Chattanooga, where they were to be discharged. What does his letter tell you about the status of the struggle at this time?

What is O'Leary's attitude toward black soldiers? The fall of Athens, Alabama, was not exactly what he had heard. About 400 black troops were captured, but some contended that the surrender had been the fault of their white commander. Nevertheless, what does O'Leary's reaction to the rumor tell you about the difficulties that blacks faced in being accepted? Also, what does this indicate about what men like O'Leary considered themselves to be fighting for?

What other evidence of disillusionment can you find in this letter? Who was the "Little Mac" whom O'Leary mentioned? How might this reference have been an indication of O'Leary's feelings about the way the war was being run? In general, what does the letter tell you about one group of Union soldiers?

Chattanooga, Tenn.

October 8th, 1864

MY DEAR WIFE

I shall endeavor to write you a few lines under difficulties. My frail canvass house is not proof against the stiff north wind that is blowing, shaking my desk so that it is almost impossible to write even if I had anything to write about. . . .

There has been some trouble along our lines of communications of late. Forrest with a large force of cavalry was between here and Nashville and deprived us of a mail for more than a week, but he had to seek other quarters in which to operate after having captured about 1,500 Negro Soldiers at Athens, Alabama. Another strong force of the enemy has been threatening the railroad between here and Atlanta, but they came to grief. They made an attack on our forces near Allatoona Mountains and were repulsed leaving 500 dead on the field. White soldiers are not so easily captured as their *colored brethren,* although Republican papers are loud in their praise of the bravery and soldierly qualities of the "down trodden African." Three railroad bridges

150

on the Atlanta road were washed away by the high water occasioned by the late heavy rains and had given us a good rest, there being no trains going from here to Atlanta, and will not be for the next week. . . .

From all accounts the draft is causing a great many to tremble in the North, who were anxious to sacrifice the last man and the last dollar to prosecute the war, but when they are called in it is quite a different thing. I will be glad to hear of some being forced to come out and enjoy the pleasure of being shot at, and see how they like it. I think their love for "Sambo" would grow small and beautifully less in a short time.

I noticed today while in town that the approaching election was the only topic of conversation among the soldiers. They seemed to be pretty equally divided but the Lincoln men made the most noise. They called their brother soldiers who were for "Little Mac" traitors to their country and anything else in that line that they could think of.

Give my love to all the family. . . . Hoping you are well and to hear from you soon I remain

your loving husband
D. O'LEARY

Courtesy of the Kentucky Historical Society, Frankfort, Kentucky.

MAP EXERCISE

Fill in or identify the following on the blank map provided. Use the maps in the text as your source.

1. States that seceded before the fall of Fort Sumter (with dates of secession).
2. States that seceded after the fall of Fort Sumter (with dates of secession).
3. Border states (slave states that did not secede).
4. Western counties of Virginia that remained loyal to the Union.
5. States involved in the campaigns.
6. Towns, cities, rivers, and streams that were principal landmarks in the campaigns.
7. Troop movements of the Union and Confederate forces, with commanders indicated.
8. Battle sites, including (a) names of the battles, (b) dates fought, and (c) the victors.

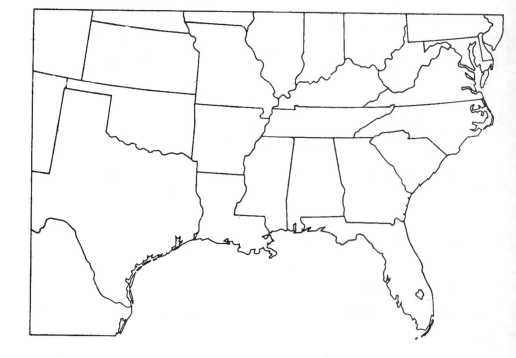

Interpretative Questions

1. Note the order in which the first seven states seceded. Now refer to the previous map on the Compromise of 1850 (see page 361) and note the percentage of the population in these states that were slaves. What does this suggest about the way the institution of slavery might have shaped Southern political attitudes?

2. Of the first seven Southern states to secede, Texas had the lowest percentage of slaves in its population (a percentage lower than some of the states that remained in the Union). What geographic factors might have worked in favor of secession in Texas? Did geographic factors influence the order of secession in the other states?

3. Why did four states that eventually seceded hesitate?

4. Why did the western counties of Virginia remain in the Union? What does this indicate about how geography shapes sociopolitical attitudes?

5. What effect did the secession of Virginia have on Union war strategy? Why was it necessary for the Union to focus so much of its attention on the Virginia theater?
6. What effect did the choice of Richmond as the capital of the Confederacy have on the South's war strategy? Why was it necessary for the South to focus so much of its attention on the Virginia theater?
7. Why did Lee invade the North in September of 1862? What engagements made this possible? What did he hope to accomplish? What was the outcome?
8. Why did Lee invade the North in the summer of 1863? What engagements made this possible? What did he hope to accomplish? What was the outcome?
9. Why were Chattanooga and Atlanta so important to the Union strategy and to Confederate hopes for winning (or at least continuing) the war?
10. What was the significance of Sherman's March to the Sea?
11. What was Lee trying to accomplish when he was cut off and forced to surrender at Appomattox? From the information on the map in the text, how realistic was his goal?

SUMMARY

Before 1860, references to the nation generally began "these United States are," but after 1865, it became more frequently "the United States is." In that change, one might well see the most important outcome of the American Civil War. The question of the nature of the Union, which had been debated since its inception, was settled—the nation was one and indivisible. The cost had been great, in both human and financial terms, but the war had done more than defeat a secessionist rebellion. It had set the nation on a new course. States' rights, as an alternative to nationalism, had been dealt a fatal blow. The tariff and internal improvements were law and would remain so. Slavery was abolished, free labor was triumphant, and industrial growth and material progress seemed to lie ahead. The war, therefore, was more than a victory for the armies of the Union—the real victor had been the Union itself. Never again would the supremacy of national laws be seriously questioned. The Civil War gave birth to the modern United States. Indeed, it did end an era and begin another.

CHAPTER SELF-TEST

After you have read the chapter in the text and done the exercises in the study guide, the following self-test can be taken to see if you understand the material you have covered. Answers appear at the end of the study guide.

Multiple Choice

Circle the letter of the response that best answers the question or completes the statement.

1. By the end of the 1850s the two-party system in the United States:
   a. was the only thing holding the nation together.
   b. still focused on the issues that had created the "second party system."
   c. had reduced slavery to a minor issue.
   d. accentuated rather than muted regional controversy.

2. Which of the following stands did President Buchanan take after the first states seceded?
   a. No state has the right to secede from the Union.
   b. The federal government has no authority to stop a state from seceding from the nation.
   c. Federal troops should be called out to stop secession.
   d. Secession was a legal act.
   e. a and b
   f. a and c

3. Which of the following was true when the Civil War began?
   a. All the important material advantages lay with the North.
   b. The South had the active support of England.
   c. Southern industry was sufficient to conduct a war.
   d. The Union was prepared for a long war.

4. Which of the following was not an advantage enjoyed by the South at the outset of the war?
   a. It would be fighting, for the most part, a defensive war.
   b. Most of the white population of the South supported the war.
   c. Northern opinion on the war was divided.
   d. All of the above

5. Which of the following was *not* enacted by the Republican Party during the Civil War?
   a. A new National Bank Act
   b. Increased taxes on almost all goods and services

154

c. Higher tariffs

d. Hard money policies requiring all payments in gold or silver

6. In which of the following acts did Lincoln "ignore" the Constitution?
    a. Sending troops into battle without asking for a declaration of war
    b. Increasing the size of the regular army
    c. Putting diplomatic pressure on England not to recognize the Confederacy
    d. Unilaterally proclaiming a naval blockade of the South

7. The Emancipation Proclamation freed slaves:
    a. in the North as well as the South.
    b. in areas of the Confederacy except those already under Union control.
    c. and offered compensation to the masters in slave states that remained loyal to the Union.
    d. in the South but offered to return them to masters who declared their loyalty to the Union.

8. The Civil War caused difficulties for American workers because it:
    a. cut off immigration and they had to work harder.
    b. drove prices up and cut purchasing power.
    c. prevented mechanization, so they had to work longer hours.
    d. removed almost all women from the workplace.

9. The Confederacy ultimately financed its war effort through:
    a. an income tax.
    b. requisitions from the states.
    c. paper money.
    d. tariffs on imported goods.

10. The greatest source of division in the South was:
    a. the doctrine of states' rights.
    b. the difference of opinion over the war.
    c. the question of whether to use slaves in combat.
    d. over King Cotton diplomacy.

11. In England, the South was supported by the:
    a. unenfranchised classes.
    b. ruling classes.
    c. Liberals.
    d. English manufacturers.

12. The United States was upset when England declared neutrality because:
    a. it meant that England might aid the South.
    b. the two sides in the conflict were of equal stature.

c. the South could easily get English loans.

d. such a declaration usually led to diplomatic recognition.

13. The first battle of the Civil War was:
    a. Shiloh.
    b. the Seven Days.
    c. First Bull Run.
    d. Wilson's Creek.

14. The bloodiest engagement of the Civil War was fought at:
    a. Antietam.
    b. Gettysburg.
    c. Atlanta.
    d. Chickamauga.

15. Sherman's march through Georgia was designed to:
    a. find supplies for the Union armies in Virginia.
    b. free the slaves in central Georgia.
    c. get Lincoln reelected.
    d. break the will of the Southern people.

True/False

Read each statement carefully. Mark true statements "T" and false statements "F."

___1. The Crittenden Compromise failed because Republicans refused to give in on the question of the expansion of slavery.

___2. Many Southerners believed that the dependence of English and French textile industries on American cotton would force them to intervene on the side of the Confederacy.

___3. The Republican Party did little to promote economic development during the war.

___4. African Americans were not allowed to serve in organized fighting units.

___5. In both the North and the South, the draft was accepted with little protest.

___6. Had the Union not taken Atlanta in September of 1864, Lincoln might have lost the presidency to McClellan.

___7. The Civil War transformed the North from an agrarian to an industrial society.

___8. The Confederate government was composed of the most radical Southern secessionists.

___9. Despite many shortages, the South was at least able to grow enough food to meet its needs.

___10. Lincoln's handling of the war effort faced constant scrutiny from the congressional Committee on the Conduct of the War, which seriously interfered with his work.

___11. Technological advances made little difference in the outcome of the Civil War, since both sides had access to them.

___12. No European nation offered diplomatic recognition to the Confederacy.

___13. Though outmanned on the land, the Confederacy held the advantage at sea.

___14. After General McClellan allowed Lee to retreat into Virginia following Antietam Creek, Lincoln removed McClellan from command.

___15. After the Battle of Chattanooga, the Confederacy's only hope was to hold on and exhaust the Northern will to fight.

Review Questions

These questions are to be answered with essays. This will allow you to explore relationships among individuals, events, and attitudes of the period under review.

1. Why did the South secede? What pushed the Southern states over the brink? Examine the events of late 1859 and 1860 in the light of Southern social and economic concerns and from the standpoint of Southern political philosophy. From this, determine why the South resorted to secession.

2. In the last chapter you assessed the "blundering generation" theory and thought about whether the Civil War was a "repressible" or an "irrepressible" conflict. After studying this chapter, revise your previous answer.

3. Some Northerners also regarded secession as an answer to the problem of slavery. Why were the majority willing to fight to hold the Union together?

4. Why did the North win? In an essay some years ago, Richard Current suggested that "God was on the side of the heaviest battalions," but is that a complete explanation? What other factors contributed to the outcome? Bring together these factors, and, after careful analysis, determine why the North did win.

CHAPTER FIFTEEN
Reconstruction and the New South

OBJECTIVES

A thorough study of Chapter 15 should enable you to understand:

1. The conditions in the former Confederacy after Appomattox that would have made any attempt at genuine reconstruction most difficult.

2. The differences between the Conservative and Radical views on the reconstruction process, and the reasons for the eventual Radical domination.

3. The functioning of the impeachment process in the case of President Andrew Johnson, and the significance of his acquittal for the future of Reconstruction.

4. Radical Reconstruction in practice, and Southern (black and white) reaction to it.

5. The debate among historians concerning the nature of Reconstruction, its accomplishments, and its harmful effects on the South.

6. The national problems faced by President Ulysses S. Grant, and the reasons for his lack of success as chief executive.

7. The diplomatic successes of the Johnson and Grant administrations, and the role of the presidents in achieving them.

8. The greenback question, and how it reflected the postwar financial problems of the nation.

9. The alternatives that were available during the election of 1876, and the effects of the so-called Compromise of 1877 on the South and on the nation.

10. The methods used by white Southerners to regain control of the region's politics.

11. The reasons for the failure of the South to develop a strong industrial economy after Reconstruction.

12. The ways in which Southerners decided to handle the race question, and the origin of the system identified with "Jim Crow."

13. The response of blacks to conditions in the South following Reconstruction.

PERTINENT QUESTIONS

The Problems of Peacemaking (pp. 398–403)

1. What effects did the Civil War have on the economy and social system of the South?
2. What special problems did the freedmen face immediately after the war? What efforts were made to help them?
3. What political implications did the readmission of the Southern states pose for the political parties, especially the Republicans?
4. What were the differences among the Conservative, Radical, and Moderate factions of the Republican Party during Reconstruction?
5. What were the objectives and provisions of Lincoln's plan for Reconstruction? How did the Radical Republicans respond to it?
6. Describe Andrew Johnson's approach to Reconstruction. How was it shaped by his political background and his personality?

Radical Reconstruction (pp. 403–408)

7. Describe the Black Codes and the congressional reaction to them. How did President Johnson respond to Congress?
8. What were the key provisions of the Fourteenth Amendment? What happened to it in 1866?
9. Explain the basic provisions of the congressional plan of Reconstruction of 1867 and tell how it was implemented. What were the implications of waiting so long after the war to get a comprehensive plan in place?
10. What measures did the Radical Republicans take to keep President Johnson and the Supreme Court from interfering with their plans? What ultimately happened to Johnson's influence?

The South in Reconstruction (pp. 408–412)

11. What three groups constituted the Republican Party in the South during Reconstruction?
12. How do the facts of political life in the Reconstruction states compare to the oft-stated white charges of corruption, black domination, and misrule?
13. What changes in Southern education began to emerge during Reconstruction? Who pushed for these changes?

14. What changes in land ownership occurred in the South after the Civil War? What pattern of land occupancy characterized most blacks in the postwar South?
15. How did the typical agricultural credit system in the postwar South affect farmers—especially poor ones?
16. What economic advances did the freedmen make? How did the economic status of blacks compare with that of the average white Southerner?
17. How did freedom affect black family life?

The Grant Administration (pp. 412–415)

18. How did Ulysses S. Grant's political accomplishments compare with his military ability?
19. What episodes led to the Liberal Republican break over "Grantism" and later to the second-term scandals?
20. People in what financial condition were most likely to favor expansion of the currency supply with greenbacks? What sparked interest in greenbacks?

The Abandonment of Reconstruction (pp. 415–419)

21. What tactics did *white* Southern Democrats use to restrict or control black suffrage?
22. Why did Northern Republicans begin to take less interest in Reconstruction and the cause of the freedmen after about 1870?
23. Why was the presidential election of 1876 disputed? How was the controversy resolved by the "Compromise of 1877"?
24. What was President Rutherford B. Hayes's objective in the South? Did he succeed?
25. Compare white and black expectations for Reconstruction with the actual results. Why were most black hopes dashed? What black gains were made?

The New South (pp. 419–426)

26. What were the typical socioeconomic and political characteristics of the "Redeemers" (Bourbons)?
27. How did the policies of the "Redeemer" governments compare with those of the Reconstruction-era administrations?
28. In what particular products was industrialization in the South most advanced? What factors attracted industrial capital to the region after the war?
29. Describe the composition of the industrial work force in the South. What was life in a mill town like?

30. Describe the typical pattern of Southern agriculture in the late nineteenth and early twentieth centuries. What problems confronted most farmers? What groups were most notably affected?
31. Describe the rise of the black middle class.
32. What was Booker T. Washington's prescription for black advancement as expressed in the "Atlanta Compromise" and elsewhere?
33. How did the civil rights cases of 1883 and *Plessy* v. *Ferguson* (1896) substantially negate the effect of the equal-protection clause of the Fourteenth Amendment?
34. What strategies and legal devices did the Southern states use to evade the spirit of the Fifteenth Amendment? What motivated the late nineteenth- and early twentieth-century crackdown on black voting?
35. Describe the pervasive nature of "Jim Crow" laws. How was the system enforced, formally and informally?
36. Explain the historic debate over Reconstruction and show how the various interpretations were reflections of the time in which they were written.

IDENTIFICATION

Identify each of the following, and explain why it is important within the context of the chapter.

1. Lincoln's plan for Reconstruction
2. O. O. Howard
3. Thaddeus Stevens
4. Charles Sumner
5. Wade-Davis Bill
6. John Wilkes Booth
7. John Hope Franklin
8. Joint Committee on Reconstruction
9. Edwin M. Stanton
10. scalawag
11. carpetbagger
12. sharecropping
13. spoils system/civil service
14. Crédit Mobilier
15. "whiskey ring"
16. Hamilton Fish
17. "Seward's Folly"

18. *"Alabama"* claims
19. "redeemed"
20. Ku Klux Klan
21. Samuel J. Tilden
22. "solid" Democratic South
23. Henry W. Grady
24. lynching

DOCUMENT

Read the portions of the chapter that discuss the Black Codes. Also read the "Debating the Past" discussion (p. 404). The following selection is taken from the writings of William A. Dunning. Consider the following questions: How does Dunning's account reveal his racist assumptions? How would accounts such as Dunning's lead white southerners in the twentieth century to conclude that they had been gravely wronged by Reconstruction? Which of the following statements is more convincing: The Black Codes were a necessary and realistic response to the situation. The Black Codes were a thinly disguised attempt to resubjugate the freedmen.

> To a distrustful northern mind such legislation could very easily take the form of a systematic attempt to relegate the freedmen to a subjection only less complete than that from which the war had set them free. The radicals sounded a shrill note of alarm. "We tell the white men of Mississippi," said the Chicago *Tribune,* "that the men of the North will convert the state of Mississippi into a frog-pond before they will allow any such laws to disgrace one foot of soil over which the flag of freedom waves." In Congress, Wilson, Sumner, and other extremists took up the cry, and with superfluous ingenuity distorted the spirit and purpose of both the laws and the law-makers of the South. The "black codes" were represented to be the expression of a deliberate purpose by the southerners to nullify the result of the war and reestablish slavery, and this impression gained wide prevalence in the North.
>
> Yet, as a matter of fact, this legislation, far from embodying any spirit of defiance towards the North or any purpose to evade the conditions which the victors had imposed, was in the main a conscientious and straightforward attempt to bring some sort of order out of the social and economic chaos which a full acceptance of the results of war and emancipation involved. In its general principle it corresponded very closely to the actual facts of the situation. The freedmen were not, and in the nature of the case could not for generations be, on the same social, moral, and intellectual plane with the whites; and this fact was recognized by constituting them a separate class in the civil order. As in general principles, so in details, the legislation was faithful on the whole to the actual conditions with which it had to deal. The restrictions in respect to bearing arms, testifying in court, and keeping labor contracts were justified by well-established traits and habits of the negroes; and the vagrancy laws dealt with problems of destitution, idleness, and vice of which no one not in the midst of them could appreciate the appalling magnitude and complexity.

William A. Dunning, *Reconstruction: Political and Economic, 1865–1877* (1907; reprint, New York: Harper & Row [Harper Torchbooks], 1962), pp. 57–58.

MAP EXERCISE

Fill in or identify the following on the blank map provided.

1. Former Confederate states.
2. First state to be readmitted, including the year.
3. Last three states to be readmitted, including the years. (Note that the other seven were readmitted in 1868.)
4. First three states to reestablish Conservative government, including the years.
5. States in which Conservative government was not reestablished until 1876.

Interpretative Questions

Based on what you have filled in, answer the following. For some of the questions you will need to consult the narrative in your text for information or explanation.

1. Note the location of the first state to be readmitted by Congress, and explain why it was restored to the Union so quickly.
2. What did the other ten states have to do to gain their readmissions in 1868–1870?

3. Note the first three states to experience the reestablishment of Conservative government and explain why the restoration of Democratic Party rule came so quickly there.

4. What forces delayed the reestablishment of the Conservative government in the other states? What episode symbolically marks the end of the Reconstruction era?

SUMMARY

The military aspect of the American Civil War lasted less than five years and ended in April 1865, but it would take another dozen years of Reconstruction to determine what the results of the war would be. The only questions clearly settled by the time of Appomattox were that the nation was indivisible and that slavery must end. The nation faced other issues with far-reaching implications. What would be the place of the freedmen in Southern society? How would the rebellious states be brought back into their "proper relationship" with the Union? The victorious North was in a position to dominate the South, but Northern politicians were not united in either resolve or purpose. For over two years after the fighting stopped, there was no coherent Reconstruction policy. Congress and the president struggled with each other, and various factions in Congress had differing views on politics, race, and union. Congress finally won control and dominated the Reconstruction process until Southern resistance and Northern ambivalence led to the end of Reconstruction in 1877. In the years that followed, a "New South" emerged, whose leaders believed the region could be modernized through industrial development. But despite their efforts the South's agricultural sector remained predominant. No economic, political, or social issue in the South could escape the race question. The Jim Crow system created by white Southerners succeeded in evading the spirit of the Fourteenth and Fifteenth Amendments, and black hopes for political equality faded. Although enormous changes had taken place, the era left a legacy of continuing racism and sectionalism.

CHAPTER SELF-TEST

After you have read the chapter in the text and done the exercises in the study guide, the following self-test can be taken to see if you understand the material you have covered. Answers appear at the end of the study guide.

Multiple Choice

Circle the letter of the response that best answers the question or completes the statement.

1. The Thirteenth Amendment to the U.S. Constitution:
   a. declared that the right to vote could not be denied on account of race.
   b. officially ended slavery.
   c. granted "citizenship" to the freedmen.
   d. provided that states could only count three-fifths (60 percent) of their black population when determining how many members they would be given in the U.S. House of Representatives.
   e. opened up the West to homesteading by African Americans.

2. The Fourteenth Amendment to the U.S. Constitution:
   a. declared that the right to vote could not be denied on account of race.
   b. officially ended slavery.
   c. granted "citizenship" to the freedmen.
   d. provided that states could only count three-fifths (60 percent) of their black population when determining how many members they would be given in the U.S. House of Representatives.
   e. opened up the West to homesteading by African Americans.

3. The Fifteenth Amendment to the U.S. Constitution:
   a. declared that the right to vote could not be denied on account of race.
   b. officially ended slavery.
   c. granted "citizenship" to the freedmen.
   d. provided that states could only count three-fifths (60 percent) of their black population when determining how many members they would be given in the U.S. House of Representatives.
   e. opened up the West to homesteading by African Americans.

4. Which faction of the Republican Party wanted Reconstruction to punish the former Confederacy, disfranchise large numbers of Southern whites, and confiscate the property of leading Confederates?
   a. Moderates
   b. Conservatives
   c. Redeemers
   d. Scalywaggers
   e. Radicals

5. Which best describes Congressional reaction to the former Confederate states that had set up new governments under Andrew Johnson's "presidential Reconstruction"?
   a. They fully accepted all of the states except Georgia and South Carolina, which had elected no blacks to office.
   b. They conditionally accepted all of the states pending the results of local and state elections.
   c. They refused to seat the senators and representatives from the states and set up a committee to investigate and advise on Reconstruction.
   d. They fully accepted all of the states west of the Mississippi River, but required new constitutions in the others.

6. The "Black Codes" were a set of regulations established by:
   a. Congress to protect the rights of the former slaves to own property and to find employment.
   b. the U.S. Supreme Court to enforce the provisions of the Thirteenth and Fourteenth Amendments to the U.S. Constitution.
   c. the Northern states to prevent a massive influx of former slaves from entering their states and seeking homes and jobs.
   d. the Southern states to promote white supremacy and to control the economic and social activities of the freedmen.

7. Which of the following, if any, was *not* a provision of the congressional plan of Reconstruction enacted in early 1867?
   a. Dividing the South into military districts administered by military commanders
   b. Requiring former Confederate states, as a condition of readmission to the Union, to ratify the Fourteenth Amendment to the U.S. Constitution
   c. Mandating former Confederate states, as a condition of readmission to the union, to hold a constitutional convention and prepare a constitution providing for black male suffrage
   d. Declaring that each state must present a plan for distributing farmland to or providing jobs for the former slaves
   e. All of the above were provisions of the congressional plan of Reconstruction

8. Critics of native Southern whites who joined the Republican Party called them:
   a. carpetbaggers.
   b. whippersnappers.
   c. scalawags.
   d. white camellias.
   e. filibusterers.

9. Which best describes the extent of "Negro rule" in the Southern states during Reconstruction?
   a. African Americans played a significant political role in several states but never elected a governor or controlled a state legislature.
   b. Some African Americans held local elective offices and a very few were elected to state legislatures but the numbers were politically inconsequential in every state.
   c. In the Deep South states where African Americans constituted a majority of the voters due to white disfranchisement, blacks dominated both houses of the state legislatures and controlled state politics as long as federal troops remained in the South.
   d. African Americans did not actually hold many offices in any state, but they effectively dominated local offices in all but Tennessee and Arkansas through alliances with white Republicans.

10. The key point of contact in the agricultural credit system for most Southern farmers, black and white, in the late nineteenth century was:
    a. small-town banks owned by Northerners.
    b. large diversified planters.
    c. finance companies in the larger cities such as Atlanta and Memphis.
    d. local country store merchants.
    e. mail-order mortgage companies operating out of New York.

11. In the late nineteenth century, the agricultural credit system in the South encouraged farmers to:
    a. rely heavily on cash crops—especially cotton.
    b. diversify away from cotton toward food grains and livestock.
    c. adopt the use of mechanization on increasingly larger farms.
    d. abandon farming and invest in capital-intensive manufacturing enterprises.

12. Ulysses S. Grant's election as president was largely a result of his being:
    a. governor of New York during the postwar economic boom.
    b. a triumphant commanding general of the Union army.
    c. the popular administrator of the Freedmen's Bureau.
    d. a flamboyant cavalry officer in the western Indian wars.

13. Which of the following, if any, was *not* associated with the "Compromise of 1877"?
    a. Removal of the last federal troops from the South
    b. Increased federal aid for railroads and other internal improvements
    c. Appointment of a Southerner to the cabinet
    d. Making Rutherford B. Hayes president
    e. All of the above are associated with the "Compromise of 1877."

14. Which of the following, if any, is *not* cited by the text as a reason that Reconstruction failed to accomplish more to promote racial equality in the United States?
    a. Fear that harsh action might lead to resumed military action by the Southern states, even though they had been defeated
    b. Attachment to a states' rights view of the Constitution, even for the rebel states
    c. Deep respect for private property rights, even for leading Confederates
    d. Belief in black inferiority by many whites, even Northern liberals
    e. All of the above were cited as reasons that Reconstruction failed to accomplish more.

15. The "solid" South refers to the:
    a. work ethic values of Southern whites.
    b. courage of Confederate soldiers during the war despite being outnumbered.
    c. steady returns that Northern bankers could expect from investment in cotton.
    d. fact that the Democratic Party could count on the votes of the Southern states after Reconstruction.

16. In most Southern states, the "Redeemers" or "Bourbons" were typically composed of:
    a. a newly emerging class of merchants, industrialists, railroad developers, and financiers.
    b. essentially the same old planter elite that had dominated antebellum politics.
    c. a coalition of poor, working-class whites and blacks.
    d. white farmers who owned small to medium farms.

17. Henry W. Grady was:
    a. the builder of the American Tobacco Company.
    b. an Atlanta editor who became a leading spokesman for the "New South" idea.
    c. the person principally responsible for Birmingham, Alabama, becoming an iron and steel production center.
    d. the governor of South Carolina who was most vociferous in advocating that blacks should migrate from the South to take industrial jobs in the North.

18. Booker T. Washington's principal message to African Americans was that they should:
    a. concentrate on practical, industrial education and work toward adopting the standards of the white middle class.
    b. join in common economic interests with white workers to bring the trade union movement to the South so that the wages would rise for all.
    c. strive first for full voting rights because only political power could bring economic gain
    d. abandon the South and seek factory jobs in the North where segregation was less of a problem.

19. "Jim Crow" is a nickname for:
    a. white Southerners who used violence or intimidation to restrict black activities.
    b. black people who curried favor with whites by acting excessively polite and deferential.
    c. the whole system of laws and customs that kept the races separate in schools, public buildings, housing, jobs, theaters, etc.
    d. black people who pretended to be friendly toward whites but who secretly undermined white interests.
    e. the African-American culture of dance, music, food, and religion that grew up after slavery.

20. In *Plessy* v. *Ferguson* (1896) the U.S. Supreme Court established the general principle that:
    a. states could not prevent blacks from voting just because their grandparents had been slaves.
    b. states could require separate accommodations on trains, in schools, etc., for blacks and whites as long as the accommodations were equal.
    c. Congress could take away a state's seats in the U.S. House of Representatives if the state refused to allow blacks to vote in congressional elections.
    d. local governments could use zoning and building codes to enforce racial segregation by neighborhood.

True/False

Read each statement carefully. Mark true statements "T" and false statements "F."

___1. As bad as the economic and physical situation was for Southern blacks in the aftermath of the Civil War, conditions were even worse for the region's white population.

___2. The Emancipation Proclamation ended slavery throughout the South in 1863.

___3. Republicans were afraid that the quick return of the Southern states to Congress would lead to more Democratic votes, thereby increasing the likelihood that Congress would establish protective tariffs and subsidize railroads.

___4. President Lincoln believed that a lenient Reconstruction policy would encourage Southern Unionists and other Southern Whigs to become Republicans and build a stronger party in the South.

___5. John Wilkes Booth acted completely on his own in plotting to murder President Lincoln.

___6. Characteristics of Andrew Johnson's personality that hampered him as president were that he was too polite and deferential to assume any leadership initiative.

___7. The Tenure of Office Act and the Command of the Army Act were passed by Congress to prevent Southern states from sending former Confederates to Congress or from having them control the state militia companies.

___8. Even though the House's impeachment charges were nominally based on specific "high crimes and misdemeanors," Andrew Johnson was actually convicted by the Senate and removed from the presidency for petty political reasons.

___9. Despite the end of slavery, most black agricultural labor in the South in the late nineteenth century continued to emulate the gang-labor system in which slaves lived in concentrated quarters and worked in groups under the constant supervision of a white field boss suggestive of the prewar overseer.

___10. During the period from just before the Civil War to just after Reconstruction, per capita income for African Americans rose significantly while per capita income for whites dropped.

___11. In the 1870s, the expanded printing of greenback paper currency was advocated by those, especially debtors, who believed that inflation would help the economy.

___12. In the context of Reconstruction, "redeemed" was used to refer to freedmen who had returned to their original slave plantations as workers after running away during or immediately following the war.

___13. The Crédit Mobilier was a railroad construction company involved in scandal during the Grant administration.

___14. Hamilton Fish was Grant's secretary of state whose action worsened relations between the United States and Great Britain.

___15. Alaska was called "Seward's Folly" because of his abortive attempt to sell the territory to the Russian czar as a method of financing the cost of maintaining troops in the South during Reconstruction.

___16. In the period from the end of Reconstruction into the twentieth century, the Democratic Party was the political party of the vast majority of Southern whites.

___17. In general, the "Redeemer" ("Bourbon") political regimes were inclined to raise taxes to expand services, especially public education.

___18. By 1900 the portion of the nation's manufacturing output produced in the South was about three times what it had been on the eve of the Civil War.

___19. The portion of Southern farmers who were tenants, cash or sharecrop, increased markedly from Reconstruction to 1900.

___20. In the period from Reconstruction to 1900, the crop-lien system helped force many Southern backcountry farmers in the piney woods and mountains from cash crop commercial farming into a ruggedly independent sort of subsistence farming.

___21. By the late 1890s, a significantly smaller portion of Southern blacks was allowed to vote than in the late 1860s.

Review Questions

These questions are to be answered with essays. This will allow you to explore relationships among individuals, events, and attitudes of the period under review.

1. Compare and contrast the several plans for Reconstruction: Lincoln's plan, the Wade-Davis Bill, Johnson's presidential Reconstruction, and the congressional plan. Consider provisions, motives, goals, and results. What forces and attitudes kept a more radical plan from being adopted?

2. Evaluate the successes and failures of Reconstruction. Given the context of the times, explain what, if anything, could have been done to avoid the failures and expand the successes. What groundwork was laid for the future?

3. Although many changes had occurred by 1900, the South remained an impoverished agricultural region, lagging well behind the rest of the nation. Describe the economic changes in the South, and assess why they were not adequate to bring the old Confederacy into the national mainstream, as some of the region's spokespersons had hoped.

4. Explain the ways in which the Southern white establishment was able to evade the spirit of the Fourteenth and Fifteenth Amendments to the Constitution. What alternative paths of accommodation and resistance did black leaders propose to this rise of Jim Crow?

Writing a Historical Book Review

Writing a book review as an assignment in a history course is designed to promote at least four important objectives: (1) effective writing, (2) substantive knowledge about a particular historical topic, (3) the development of a historical perspective and an understanding of the nature and use of historical research, and (4) an ability to think critically about the work of others. A typical summary "book report" can at best teach only the first two objectives. A critical book review goes beyond mere summary to inquire into the overall worth of the work. There are six steps to preparing a review of a historical work. With some modifications, these steps also apply to writing reviews of other nonfiction works.

1.   *Select a book.*
Your instructor may provide a reading list, but if he or she does not, you will find that locating an appropriate work can be a very important part of the learning process. Start, of course, with the Suggested Readings at the end of each chapter in your text and with the book catalog (computer-based or cards) in your college library. Check standard bibliographies such as *Harvard Guide to American History,* and try consulting the footnotes or bibliographies of other works. When you locate a likely book, give it a quick once-over. Glance at the table of contents and the bibliography, and read the prefatory material to make sure that the book is appropriate for your assignment. Ask yourself if the topic seems interesting, for you will probably write a better review if you have some affinity for the subject. Most importantly, talk to your instructor; he or she has read many books and has probably graded hundreds of reviews, so seek your instructor out for advice.

2.   *Determine the purpose of the book and the intended audience.*
The best place to determine both purpose and audience is usually in the preface, foreword, or introduction. What demand did the author intend to fulfill with the book? Did the author write because there was no satisfactory work available on the subject? Did the writer feel that he or she had a new point of view on a well-worn topic? Perhaps the author wrote a popular account of a subject about which previous works had been dull and dry. Ascertaining the author's purpose is important, for, assuming that the purpose is worthwhile, the writer should be judged by whether he or she achieved what they set out to accomplish. Also

determine the audience for which the work was intended. Was the work directed mainly at professional historians, at college students, or at the general public?

3.   *Learn the author's qualifications and viewpoint.*
Find out the author's academic background. Is the author a journalist, a professor, or a professional writer? Has this writer published other books on related topics? Consult your library catalog; check *Who's Who in America, Contemporary Authors, Directory of American Scholars,* or other directories. Viewpoint, however, is generally more important than credentials, since an author must be judged mainly by the quality of the particular work you are examining. A Pulitzer Prize winner may later write an undistinguished book. But many first books, often derived from the author's doctoral dissertation, are outstanding. Knowing the author's point of view, however, may put a reader on guard for certain biases. A Marxist historian will often write from a predictable perspective, as will an extreme rightist. Biographers are often biased for or against their subjects. For example, after the assassination of John F. Kennedy, many of his intimates, most notably Arthur Schlesinger, Jr., wrote biographical works. A reviewer could not adequately analyze Schlesinger's *Thousand Days* without knowing something about his close relationship with the slain president. Look for information on point of view in prefatory materials, in the body of the book, and in reference works with entries about the author.

4.   *Read the book.*
Read critically and analytically. Be sure to identify the author's thesis—the main argument of the book. Look for secondary theses and other important points. See how the author uses evidence and examples to support arguments. Are his or her sources adequate and convincing? Does the author rely mainly on primary— firsthand, documentary—sources or on secondary sources? Consider the author's style and presentation. Is the book well organized? Is the prose lively, direct, and clear? Take notes as you read so that you can return to particularly important passages or especially revealing quotations. Remember that being critical means being rational and thoughtful, not necessarily negative.

5.   *Outline the review.*
The following outline is only a suggestion; it is not a model that you should necessarily follow for all reviews. You may find it appropriate to add, combine, separate, eliminate, or rearrange some points.

I. Introduction

    A. Purpose of the book

    B. Author's qualifications and viewpoint

II. Critical summary

    A. Thesis of the book

    B. Summary of contents, indicating how the thesis is developed (Use examples. While this will generally be the longest part of the review, you should make sure that your paper does not become a mere summary without critical analysis.)

    C. Author's use of evidence to support the thesis and secondary points

III. Style and presentation

    A. Organization of the book

    B. Writing style (word choice, paragraph structure, wit, readability, length, etc.)

    C. Use of aids (photographs, charts, tables, figures, etc.)

IV. Conclusion

    A. Historical contribution of the book (How does the book fit into the prevailing interpretation of the topic? Does it break new ground? Does it answer a troublesome question? Does it revise older interpretations? Does it merely clarify and simplify the standard point of view? You may need to consult other sources when considering this point. See, for example, the "Debating the Past" sections in your text.)

    B. Overall worth of the book (Would you recommend it? For what type of audience would it be best suited? Did the author accomplish the intended purpose?)

6.   *Write the review.*

Follow your outline. Use standard written English. When in doubt, consult *The McGraw-Hill College Handbook* or a similar reference. If your instructor does not assign a standard format, the following style is accepted.

I.   At the top of the first page, give the standard bibliographic citation of the work under review. (Reviews seldom have titles of their own.)

II.   The review should be printed double-spaced on good-quality paper. The typical review is from 450 to 1,200 words long.

III.   If you quote from the book under review, simply follow the quotation with the page number(s) in parentheses. For example: "The author makes the incredible assertion, 'Jefferson turned out to be America's worst president' (p. 345)."

IV.   If you need to cite other sources for quotations, points of view, or facts, use a standard citation style.

You may find it helpful to read published book reviews as a guide to the preparation of your own review. Most historical journals, including the *American Historical Review* and the *Journal of American History,* publish many short reviews at the end of each issue. *Reviews in American History,* which prints longer reviews, is especially useful. To determine where reviews of the particular book you have chosen have been published, consult the *Book Review Digest* or the *Book Review Index.* Assume that your audience is college educated and well read, but do not assume that your hypothetical reader has in-depth knowledge about the subject of the book under review.

Preparing a Historical Research Paper

A research paper helps students develop competencies very much like those that are enhanced by doing a book review. One of the best ways to develop a historical perspective is to actually write some history, even a short research essay. In addition, preparing a paper gives students the opportunity to become more competent in research skills and in the organization of diverse materials into a meaningful essay. The suggestions that follow are of a general nature, designed to enable an instructor to adapt them to the kind of project that best suits the class. These suggestions are directed to students taking the introductory course who may be writing their first historical research papers at the college level.

1.   *Select a topic.*
This should be done with the advice of the instructor. Many instructors have a list of suitable topics to offer their students. If no such list exists, you should consider the following questions: (a) Will the topic help you understand the course? (b) Can a paper on the topic be finished during the term? (Students often bite off more than they can chew. It is better to select a manageable topic, such as "Lincoln's Veto of the Wade-Davis Bill," than one such as "Abraham Lincoln: President.") (c) Is sufficient material available to do an adequate job of research? (d) Does the topic interest you? There are, of course, other factors to consider, but if the answer to any of the above is "no," then the value of the project is lessened considerably.

2.   *Locate sources.*
Sources for a research paper fall into two general categories: (a) *primary material*—sources produced by people who took part in or witnessed the events being researched (letters, diaries, pictures, newspaper accounts, and so forth); and (b) *secondary material*—sources produced after the fact and generally written relying on the primary sources. To locate these sources, you should first consult a bibliographic guide, such as the *Harvard Guide to American History* or *American History and Life.* This will enable you to identify a number of secondary sources whose bibliographies give you more material (primary and secondary) to look into. You should also examine historical journals, particularly those that concentrate on the field into which your topic falls. You

should read related articles, paying attention to the sources they cite, and book reviews, which will tell you of new works on the subject. Once a source is located, you should write its full bibliographic citation on an index card or in a form appropriate to your software. This will make it easier to organize your bibliography during the hectic days just before the paper is due. Consult *The McGraw-Hill College Handbook* for examples of bibliographic and footnote form. Most colleges have collections of primary material—on microfilm or printed—to aid students in this kind of research. Be sure to remember that you must give citations for material located via the Internet or World Wide Web just as you would those found in a traditional library. If the source is one generally available in printed version, such as a historical journal, provide normal citation followed by a notation that it was cited from the on-line version. If the source is only available on-line, cite the sponsoring entity and give the Internet or Web address.

3.   *Do the research.*

The research process has as many approaches as there are researchers, but until you develop the method best suited to you, here are some helpful hints. Begin by reading general accounts of the circumstances surrounding the topic you have chosen. For example, if your topic is "Witch Trials at Salem," read a general study of late-seventeenth-century Massachusetts. Then turn to the more specific secondary sources. (Consult the Suggested Readings at the end of each chapter in the text for background sources.) Take notes on index cards, one citation to each card (or the software equivalent). In this way, you will have notes that can be arranged in the order you desire when the time comes to write. Do not worry about having too many notes. It is better to have too many than too few, which would mean additional research at the last minute. Also, when taking notes, be sure to record the location (title, volume, page) so that you will not have to backtrack to find a citation. If you do the work the first time, you will not have to waste time retracing your steps at the end.

4.   *Organize the paper.*

If your research is done systematically, the organization of the paper will all but take care of itself. There are, however, a few hints that might be helpful. First, do not leave this to be done last. Even while you are pulling material together, you should be organizing it into a loose outline. This will show you where gaps exist and reveal which areas need work, and will often cause you to redirect your efforts in a more productive way. In this way, the process of organizing is ongoing, and so when the research is done, the paper is organized. Still, you should prepare a final outline just before you begin to write. This forces you to go over all the material once again, makes it fresh in your mind, and gives you the opportunity to make any last-minute adjustments.

5.   *Write the paper.*

Again, if the previous steps have been carefully taken, writing the paper is easy. The notes you have accumulated should be organized to correspond with your outline. However, be sure to pay attention to your thesis so that the paper will not be just a string of notes. Write a rough draft of the paper, with documentation on a separate page. At this stage, citations may be in an abbreviated form, but they should be complete enough for later reference. Beware of the tendency to overuse quotations. As a general rule, you should quote only when the actual wording is as important as the idea being transmitted or when "colorful language" spices up the narrative. In most cases, however, it is best simply to put the information in your own words and cite the source.

For general information on the use of the language, consult *The McGraw-Hill College Handbook* or another handbook used in freshman English classes.

6.   *Prepare the final draft*

After the rough draft is finished and at least one revision has taken place, the clean copy should be prepared. Notes may be placed at the bottom of each page, at the back, or in the narrative, depending on the instructor's preference. The bibliography should be placed at the end of the paper. Other additions—title page, table of contents, an outline—may be included or omitted as the instructor desires.

By paying careful attention to the directions given by your instructor and by following the portions of this guide that apply to the project you undertake, you should develop basic research and writing competencies that will help you in many other classes.

Answers to Self-Test Questions

Chapter 1

Multiple Choice

1. c	5. a	9. b	13. c
2. d	6. b	10. b	14. b
3. a	7. a	11. a	15. b
4. c	8. c	12. d	

True-False

1. False	6. False	11. False	15. True
2. True	7. True	12. False	16. False
3. False	8. False	13. True	17. True
4. True	9. True	14. False	18. True
5. True	10. False		

Chapter 2

Multiple Choice

1. b	5. d	9. b	13. b
2. a	6. e	10. a	14. a
3. c	7. b	11. a	15. a
4. b	8. c	12. d	

True-False

1. False	5. False	9. True	13. False
2. True	6. False	10. False	14. True
3. True	7. True	11. False	15. False
4. False	8. False	12. False	16. False

Chapter 3

Multiple Choice

1. c	5. d	9. b	13. b
2. c	6. a	10. a	14. d
3. c	7. a	11. c	15. a
4. d	8. a	12. d	

True-False

1. True	5. True	9. False	13. False
2. False	6. False	10. True	14. True
3. False	7. True	11. False	15. True
4. False	8. False	12. True	

Chapter 4

Multiple Choice

1. a	5. c	9. c	13. a
2. b	6. d	10. c	14. d
3. c	7. a	11. a	15. b
4. d	8. a	12. b	16. a

True-False

1. False	5. False	9. False	13. False
2. True	6. False	10. False	14. False
3. False	7. False	11. True	15. True
4. True	8. True	12. True	

Chapter 5

Multiple Choice

1. b	5. b	9. b	13. a
2. d	6. d	10. a	14. c
3. c	7. c	11. c	15. b
4. c	8. a	12. d	

True-False

1. False	5. False	9. False	13. False
2. False	6. False	10. True	14. True
3. False	7. False	11. True	15. False
4. True	8. True	12. False	

Chapter 6

Multiple Choice

1. a	5. a	9. d	13. d
2. c	6. d	10. d	14. b
3. b	7. a	11. a	15. d
4. c	8. e	12. a	

True-False

1. True	5. False	9. True	13. False
2. True	6. True	10. True	14. False
3. True	7. True	11. True	15. True
4. False	8. False	12. True	

Chapter 7

Multiple Choice

1. b	7. a	13. d	19. d
2. d	8. d	14. a	20. b
3. a	9. b	15. b	21. a
4. b	10. a	16. b	22. a
5. b	11. b	17. a	23. a
6. c	12. c	18. c	24. c
			25. a

True-False

1. True	7. True	13. False	19. False
2. True	8. False	14. False	20. False
3. False	9. False	15. False	21. False
4. False	10. False	16. False	22. True
5. True	11. True	17. False	23. False
6. False	12. False	18. False	24. False
			25. False

Chapter 8

Multiple Choice

1. c	5. a	9. c	13. a
2. d	6. a	10. b	14. a
3. c	7. a	11. d	15. d
4. b	8. c	12. e	

True-False

1. True	5. False	9. True	13. True
2. True	6. True	10. False	14. False
3. True	7. False	11. False	
4. True	8. False	12. False	

Chapter 9

Multiple Choice

1. c	5. a	9. a	13. b
2. a	6. c	10. b	14. c
3. b	7. d	11. b	15. d
4. c	8. a	12. d	

True-False

1. False	5. False	9. False	13. True
2. True	6. False	10. True	14. True
3. False	7. True	11. False	15. False
4. False	8. True	12. True	16. True
			17. False

Chapter 10

Multiple Choice

1. f	6. b	11. a	15. c
2. a	7. a	12. b	16. a
3. a	8. b	13. d	17. d
4. b	9. c	14. b	18. e
5. d	10. c		

True-False

1. True	5. False	9. False	13. False
2. False	6. True	10. False	14. True
3. True	7. True	11. False	15. True
4. True	8. True	12. False	

Chapter 11

Multiple Choice

1. c	5. b	9. b	13. a
2. b	6. d	10. a	14. d
3. d	7. c	11. c	15. d
4. c	8. c	12. b	

True-False

1. False	5. False	9. False	13. True
2. True	6. False	10. True	14. False
3. True	7. False	11. False	15. True
4. True	8. False	12. False	16. True

Chapter 12

Multiple Choice

1. d	5. d	9. b	13. a
2. b	6. a	10. a	14. c
3. c	7. a	11. c	15. b
4. c	8. d	12. d	

True-False

1. False	5. True	9. False	13. False
2. True	6. True	10. False	14. False
3. False	7. True	11. True	15. True
4. True	8. False	12. False	

Chapter 13

Multiple Choice

1. a	5. b	9. a	13. e
2. b	6. b	10. a	14. c
3. d	7. c	11. a	
4. d	8. b	12. a	

True-False

1. True	5. False	9. False	13. True
2. False	6. False	10. False	14. False
3. False	7. True	11. True	15. True
4. True	8. True	12. True	16. False

Chapter 14

Multiple Choice

1. d	5. d	9. c	13. c
2. e	6. c	10. a	14. a
3. a	7. b	11. b	15. d
4. d	8. b	12. b	

True-False

1. True	5. False	9. False	13. False
2. True	6. True	10. True	14. True
3. False	7. False	11. False	15. True
4. False	8. False	12. True	

Chapter 15

Multiple Choice

1. b	6. d	11. a	16. a
2. c	7. d	12. b	17. b
3. a	8. c	13. e	18. a
4. e	9. a	14. a	19. c
5. c	10. d	15. d	20. b

True-False

1. False	6. False	11. True	16. True
2. False	7. False	12. False	17. False
3. False	8. False	13. True	18. False
4. True	9. False	14. False	19. True
5. False	10. True	15. False	20. False
			21. True